"A Hastiness of Cooks"

ALSO BY CYNTHIA D. BERTELSEN
Mushroom: A Global History

"A Hastiness of Cooks"

A Practical Handbook
for Use in Deciphering the Mysteries
of Historic Recipes and Cookbooks,
For Living-History Reenactors,
Historians, Writers, Chefs,
Archæologists,
and, of Course, Cooks

Cynthia D. Bertelsen

Illustrations by Courtney Nzeribe

Turquoise Moon Press

"A Hastiness of Cooks"

A Practical Handbook
for Use in Deciphering the Mysteries
of Historic Recipes and Cookbooks,
For Living-History Reenactors,
Historians, Writers, Chefs,
Archaeologists,
and, of Course, Cooks

ISBN 978-0-692-19557-4
Turquoise Moon Press
Gainesville, Florida
turquoisemoonpress.com

Dedication
To Mike, always and forever

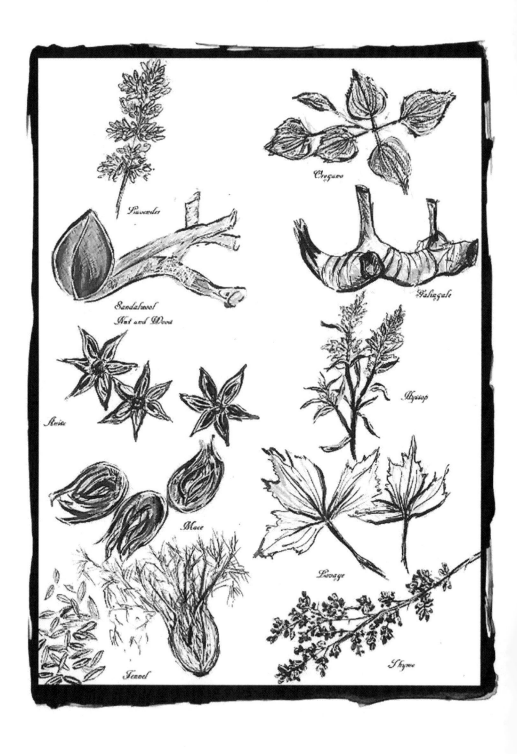

Lavender

Oregano

Sandalwood
Nut and Wood

Galangale

Anise

Hyssop

Mace

Lovage

Fennel

Thyme

About the phrase *"A Hastiness of Cooks"*

A word game, popular in the great households of late medieval England, had at its heart the creation of collective nouns. In the lists of these names, alongside the laughter of hostellers, the glossing of taverners, the promise of tapsters and the fighting of beggars, were household references – a carve of pantlers (who looked after the bread), a credence of servers, ('credence' was the process of tasting or 'assaying' foods against poison), a provision of stewards of household – and a hastiness of cooks. The pressures of the medieval kitchen, the precipitate hurry and irritation of the cooks are all captured in the medieval meanings of 'hastiness'.

~ C. M. Woolgar, The Culture of Food in England, 1200 - 1500

A Welcoming Hearth does the Heart Good

Table of Contents

Acknowledgements 15

Preface 17

Introduction: Food is Life 19

Part I: The Mysteries in Cookbooks 23

Chapter 1: In the Beginning 25

Chapter 2: What is a Cookbook? What is a Recipe? 29

Chapter 3: Why Use Cookbooks in Historical Research? 31

Part II: What's Past is Prologue 35

Chapter 4: A Very, Very Brief History of European Cookbooks 37

Chapter 5: Historic Cookbooks in England 47

Chapter 6: Historic Cookbooks in Spain 53

Part III: Theories Behind Historic Cookbook Analysis 59

Chapter 7: Living History: Using Cookbooks
in Historical Research 61

Chapter 8: Cookbook Analysis: What is Your Question? 65

Chapter 9: How to Begin: Step-by-Step Analysis
of Historic Cookbooks 67

Chapter 10: Getting Started with Recipe Reconstruction:
The Basics 77

Chapter 11: Using Fire in Recreating Historic Recipes 85

Part IV: The Practical: Recreating Historic Recipes 91

Chapter 12: Step-by-Step Analysis: Spanish Cookbooks 93

Chapter 13: Step-by-Step Analysis: English Cookbooks. 131

Part V: Tools for Background Research 163

Chapter 14: The Importance of Bibliographies. 165

Chapter 15: Online Tools 169

Chapter 16: A Final Word 175

Endnotes 177

Appendix 183

Selected Bibliographical Resources 190

Illustrations 206

Index 207

About the Author 215

About the Illustrator. 215

Acknowledgements

This book began as a celebration of remembrance for my childhood friend, Meli Duran Kirkpatrick, who journeyed on while still too young. It seemed appropriate—since we both loved food—to write something about cooking in conjunction with Meli's profession of archaeology. Meli's husband, Dr. David Kirkpatrick, encouraged me to write about using historic cookbooks in conjunction with archaeological research. I thank him for permission to include material from an article published in *Artifact*. [1]

I also thank my preliminary readers for their astute comments and feedback: Marcia Krause Bilyk, Cathy Branciaroli, David Kirkpatrick, Janet Perlman, Liz Pollack, and Laurel Robertson. A huge thanks to Ria Leonard and Gary Allen, too, for their close reads and perceptive comments.

Rachel Laudan deserves many thanks as well, for her constant support and encouragement over the years. Barbara Ketchum Wheaton admitted me to her seminar, "Reading Historic Cookbooks: A Structured Approach" at Harvard University in 2011. That experience sharpened my appreciation of historic culinary works.

Without the assistance of Cathy Gibbons Reedy, design and layout artist par excellence, this book would not have taken the shape it has.

I owe a never-ending debt to Courtney Nzeribe, too, for the magnificent illustrations that she produced for this book.

I've never met Chef Grant Achatz of Chicago's Alinea restaurant, but some words of his inspired me as I wrote this book. When it comes to the life of a creative, he quipped, "Rules? There are no rules. Do whatever you want." I hold this thought when the writing life becomes a bit overwhelming.

And, of course, my deepest thanks go to my husband Mike who, as always, stood by me through all the ups and downs.

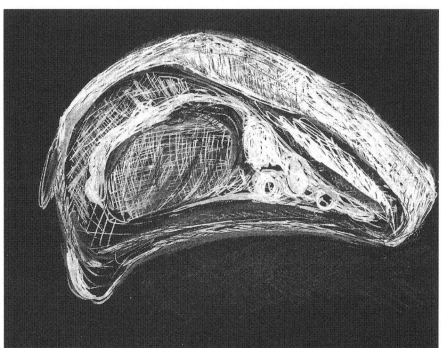

A Hunk of Beef and Piece of Pork Pie Make the Day

Preface

You'll find many cookbooks today filled with recreated, or "redacted," recipes. But perhaps the process of recreating these recipes yourself seems out of reach. Examining the original sources, deciphering the archaic language, gleaning the essence of kitchens past, well, it can be a bit much.

That's why I've written this handbook.

The books discussed here circumscribe the period from approximately 1390 A.D. to 1800 A.D. These particular texts hail from what is now England and Spain. By the time you've finished reading *A Hastiness of Cooks*, you will be able to 1) recreate period recipes and 2) analyze the subtexts of historic cookbooks.

Vast numbers of historic cookbooks—both online and in print, usually rendered as facsimiles—are available to you. This short book could not begin to discuss them all. The Selected Bibliographical Resources and Online Tools sections take up the slack and provide you much meat (or vegetable) for further study. And cooking!

Note that I've used the terminology "recreation" and "reconstruction" rather than "redaction." All translations are my own, as are any errors.

Cynthia Bertelsen
Gainesville, Florida
February 2019

"D" is for Deer and Delicious Venison Roasts

Introduction

Food is Life.

I once stood on a busy street corner in Puebla, Mexico. A market day, a late October morning, battleship-gray skies overhead. Women—young, old, rich, poor—lugged string bags or baskets laden with food, hurrying home to cook *almuerzo*, lunch.

As I watched this scene, I couldn't get the thought out of my head: Food *is* life.

Life revolves around the growing of food, the eating of it, the cooking of it. It's the saga that drives everything, including history. As Kristine Kowalchuk so perceptively puts it in *Preserving on Paper* (2017), "They [bread and wine] mean, literally life over death. Medieval and Renaissance people, because of their connection to the land and cyclical conception of time, perceived this deeper literal meaning." [2]

The script of life is all about eating to survive, to go on living. Everything humans do ultimately circles around food and the getting of it. That day in Mexico I deemed this truism an epiphany. And I still do.

Food. Such a small word with such a large meaning.

What happened after 1492 changed the world forever. Sea voyages first sponsored by the Portuguese and Spanish crowns, and later by England's Virgin Queen Elizabeth I fueled the rise of immense empires. Adding to the richness of this story are many subtexts: cultural clashes, political power, greed for gold and spices. And hegemony.

Yet something else took place, much more subtly. The diffusion of foodstuffs from across the oceans, from all the fields and forests and rivers of newly discovered lands, all that changed the world every bit as much as did all the political jockeying in the royal courts of Europe.

This handbook takes you on a whirlwind tour of historic cookbooks dating from the earliest days of cookbook writing in Europe, circa 1390, with the emergence of the English manuscript, *The Forme of Cury*, and the Catalan *Llibre de Sent Soví*. I include medieval and colonial-era Spain, because Spanish cookbooks tend not to be analyzed and studied as much as those originating in England or France or Italy. But my approach is fitting. Over a period of almost 800 years, Islamic rulers controlled much of what is now modern Spain. Influential thirteenth-century Arabic manuscripts such as *Kitâb al-Tabîkh fi'l-Maghrib wa'l-Andalus fi'asr al-Muwahhidin* (Anonymous Andalusian) and *Fudalat al-Khiwan* (The Delights of the Table) guided Spanish cookbook authors for centuries. The Arab influence on Spanish cuisine, and indeed much of medieval cooking, is undeniable.

I regard cookbooks to be primary sources as much as are culinary manuscripts or other materials. My focus here is on manuscripts and books ranging from medieval times to the end of the 1700s. All reveal information useful to archaeologists, historians, writers, reenactors, living-history interpreters, chefs, home cooks, and anyone intent on deciphering and recreating the intricacies of food history and culture.

What you'll learn from this book:

   🐚 What cookbooks teach about past social, economic, political factors

   🐚 Why it's important to know about the history of cookbooks

   🐚 How to read, interpret, and recreate recipes from period cookbooks

   🐚 Where to find information for further study

Spain ruled the New World from 1492 to 1899. At one point, England controlled 25% of world's land mass and the people therein. These empires molded the lives of both elites and ordinary people. Both of these culinary legacies still shape the historical landscape, in the same way that a river flows and cuts through rock, carving new formations.[3]

It's quite a story. Shall we begin?

Game Birds Sweeten the Pot

Part I

The Mysteries in Cookbooks

Cookbook Histories Can be as Complex as a Family Tree!

Chapter 1

In the Beginning

Smoke from the tortilla vendor's fire wafted across reddish cobblestones smeared with horse dung. Sebastian leaned over the balcony, yelling, "Don Diego, up here, here," as Don Diego de Vargas dashed along Calle de Donceles.

"*Buenos días*, Don Diego! I have that book you requested last year. This year's *flota* arrived three weeks ago and the mules brought my boxes up from Veracruz. Finally." Sebastian grinned at Don Diego. "And there're some other treasures I know you'll want to see. I'll be right down."

Although that's a fictitious account, something like it could explain how Francisco Martínez Montiño's *Arte de Cozina* ended up in Santa Fe, New Mexico. A notary listed such a book among items inventoried after Governor Diego de Vargas's death in 1704.[4]

Booksellers in colonial Mexico City sold the original 1611 edition of Martínez Montiño's cookbook. No doubt that's how Don Diego de Vargas picked up his copy—before his mule train headed north to Santa Fe—where he was to serve as governor, living high on the hog in the Palace of the Governors. Or as high as it was possible in that rather unwelcoming and unforgiving land, populated by rattlesnakes as thick as a strong man's arm and hostile Apaches rightfully resentful of the Spanish presence.

A continent away, ships from England delivered a multitude of Hannah Glasse's bestseller, *The Art of Cookery, Made Plain and Easy*, to booksellers in Williamsburg, Virginia and Boston, Massachusetts. Prior to Glasse's book, Gervase Markham's *The English Hus-wife* (1615) held pride of place in many kitchens, because "women's work was of course seriously related to survival." [5] And Markham's book appeared in the manifest of the ship *Supply*, bound for Jamestown, Virginia. [6]

E. Smith's *The Complete Housewife* (1728), too, met the needs of cooks in colonial British America, until a printer by the name of William Parks pirated the book in 1742 and issued it from his print shop in Williamsburg, Virginia. [7]

Whatever the cookbook, whatever the period of written history, for those interested in how people cooked, feasted or starved, there's gold in those scrolls and pages. The challenge is to know how to look, how to spot the telltale detail, how to dig deep into the text for subtle meanings. In a way, you'll be applying forensic linguistics to the pages in front of you, solving puzzles and answering questions.

Culinary historians often turn to archaeological research reports to better interpret the many aspects of food usage and cooking throughout history. The reverse could be true as well for archaeologists. The residue caked on the bottom of cooking pots, the telltale signs of malnutrition or disease in skeletal remains, and the odd-shaped tool near the charred hearth, all might come to life when viewed through the lens of cookbooks such as *Arte de Cozina* or *The Art of Cookery, Made Plain and Easy*.

Before delving into such culinary masterpieces as those of Martínez Montiño and Hannah Glasse, and others like them, let's take a couple of short side trips.

Don Diego de Vargas, Governor of New Mexico, also the Marqués de la Nava de Barcinas

27

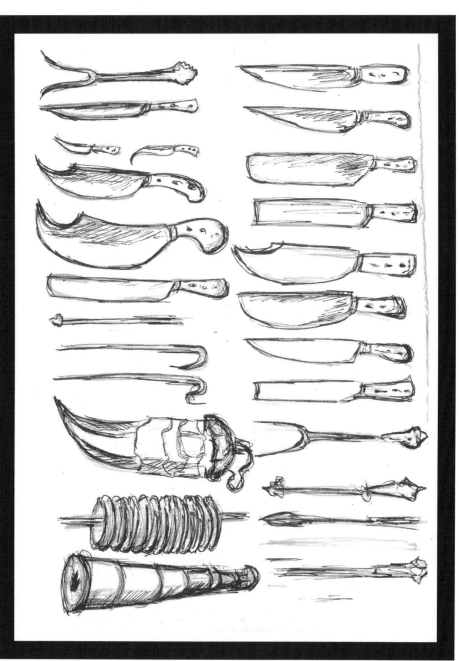

Chapter 2

What Is A Cookbook?
What Is A Recipe?

O f course, you know what a cookbook is, yes? A book of recipes. But not always.

Prolific culinary bibliographer Henry Notaker suggests that two-thirds of a cookbook ought to consist of material pertaining to food, with 40-50 percent of that in the form of "receipts," or recipes in today's terminology.[8] In many cases, cookbooks of the past contained large numbers of medicinal receipts as well as instructions for food preparation. Early cookery manuscripts often appeared in different versions, depending upon the tastes and desires of the prospective buyer.

Here's Merriam-Webster's take on the word:

[1]cook·book

noun \ ˈkůk-ˌbůk\

: a book of recipes : a book of directions explaining how to prepare and cook various kinds of food

Another Webster, *Merriam-Webster's Collegiate Dictionary*, defines a cookbook as being "a book of cooking directions and recipes." The *Oxford English Dictionary* reveals that the word "cookbook," or "cook-book," stems from American usage from around 1809, coined by a certain R. Tyler of London's Yankey district, when referring to cookery books. Prior to that, British usage included the word "cookery," often written as "cokery" or "cookry." Cookery thereby signifies "The art or practice of cooking, the preparation of food by means of fire." [9]

In other words, cookbooks provide a collection of recipes, including instructions and information about preparing and serving food and/or concocting medicines and other household necessities. Cookbooks also chronicle the cultural artifacts surrounding cooking. Most literate societies boast of a culinary canon, which—in the beginning—flowed primarily from the pens of aristocratic men who often never set foot in a kitchen.

You may notice that the contents of many old cookbooks seem to be very, very similar. And you'd be right. One word sums up this state of affairs: plagiarism. Perhaps "borrowing" or "sharing" would do as well. As you will see, cookbooks developed, at least in Europe, from certain "mothers," or roots, to grow and branch out, just as does a family tree. European cuisines tended to be quite similar to each other in those days.

Here's a definition of plagiarism, just to keep things in perspective:

Plagiarism involves the use of another's work and presenting it as one's own, without attribution or other acknowledgement of the source of the ideas or material included in one's work.

Think about it: with the coming of the book, possessing and accessing knowledge no longer required the physical presence of learned/knowledgeable people to share or pass on information/skills. To phrase it another way, the words and ideas of thinkers could move from place to place and couldn't be halted by geographical location or the chains and prison cells that held— and attempted to silence—dissidents and heretics. That said, over 75 percent of the earliest printed books continued to deal with religious, not secular, subjects. Henry Notaker suggests that only 100 "different [cookbook] titles" appeared between the 1470s and 1700. [10]

As you immerse yourself into the world of historic cookbooks, you'll essentially be exploring the history of modern humans.

Chapter 3

Why Use Cookbooks In Historical Research?

Before writing and literacy became common, people relied on oral culture. The first cookbooks took form by word-of-mouth instructions passed from mother to daughter, father to son, across generations and within work groups such as guilds[11] from one person to another. Cookery manuscripts often appeared as scrolls, but also in codex format.

Researchers read cookbooks in several ways. In examining period cookbooks, whether printed or in unpublished manuscript form, you'll find evidence illuminating several of the following points:

- Family size
- Societal changes
- Literacy and mathematical skills
- Technological changes
- Gender roles
- Religious proscriptions (fast and feast days)
- Ingredients available locally
- Ingredients acquired through trade
- Cooking equipment

- Meal patterns and other food-related behavior
- Medicinal beliefs and practices
- Upper-class values or other status markers
- Middle-class and lower-class social aspirations
- Traditions
- Geographical origins of dishes and ingredients
- Author's motivation for writing
- Patronage by celebrated and wealthy people

Language metamorphizes quickly, very quickly. Textual analysis defines and illustrates much more than mere recipes. Any recipe reconstruction must take into consideration the same issues that plague translators of any text. Unless you're working with a recent work, the language of a text reflects its time period.

Cookbooks make concrete what is basically oral culture. In many areas of the world, and during many periods of history as well, cookbooks were (and are) as scarce as hens' teeth. When people, mostly men, recorded bits and pieces about food, something compelled them to do so. Whatever their motives, such material provides historians and historical archaeologists with another tool useful in the search for the nebulous past.

De Honesta voluptate (1465), the first printed cookbook, compiled by Vatican librarian Bartolomeo Sacchi di Piadena, or Platina, led the way for many of those that followed.

Cookbooks often provide the one written source available to you concerning food practices and ingredients of a time period. A careful examination of the words used often indicate what tools may have been chosen to achieve a desired dish or taste.

While living in France, food-history scholar Barbara K. Wheaton realized the importance of cookbooks in the interpretation of daily life in early France.

She produced *Savoring the Past: The French Kitchen and Table from 1300 to 1789* (1983), a work that still provides a deep and thorough analysis of France's role in the development of European cuisines.[12] Wheaton found encouragement in the work of historians such as Fernand Braudel, whose *Annales: Economies, societés, civilizations* first appeared in 1929, a journal that continues to be published to this day. A wealth of current scholarship suggests that food studies, including studies of cookbooks, now ranks closely to other respected academic disciplines such as chemistry, engineering, history, anthropology, and archaeology.[13]

Archaeologist Elizabeth M. Scott, like Wheaton, examined cookbooks from a Eurocentric point of view, in her case British culture. In her article " 'A Little Gravy in the Dish and Onions in a Tea Cup': What Cookbooks Reveal about Material Culture," she focused on cookbooks from the 1700s and 1800s. Scott concluded that "... since functional typologies have been called into question for AngloAmerican households, we [archaeologists] should be even more cautious when assigning function to artifacts from households of other ethnic and racial groups. It is clear that established methodologies, interpretation of vessel use, status studies, and analyses of gendered labor roles all need thoughtful, critical reconsideration."[14]

Cookbooks reflect many facets of human culture, but do not necessarily record what people ate. Therefore, you must take cookbooks with a proverbial grain of salt. According to Tom Jaine of Prospect Books, a gap exists between what the historic cookery books portrayed versus what people cooked and devoured every day. This trend has been around since the beginning of cookbook printing and continues to this day. Think of glossy monthly magazines and other publications. You might drool over glorious photographs of dishes, but you will probably not make more than once. If ever.

The following discussion attempts to clarify the potential worth of cookbooks in any historical study. Whether you are an historical archaeologist faced with puzzling items of material culture, a chef or caterer interested in cooking historical dishes, a novelist or writer wishing to include details about food in stories, a reenactor/living-history performer researching and presenting workshops, or an adventurous home cook with a penchant for history, this book will help you in recreating approximations of the dishes eaten by people in times past.

By using examples from selected cookbooks pertaining to Spain and England, you will get a handle on the basic process necessary to decipher all those ambiguous and mysterious recipes. And their subtexts.

At the end of your quest, you may not find the fabled city of El Dorado, nor the Holy Grail, but nonetheless cookbooks such as these reveal a treasure trove of material for all manners of culinary endeavors.

Spain

The Book of Sent Soví (14th C)

Libre de Guisados (1525)

Libro del Arte de Cozina (1607)

Arte de Cozina (1611)

Nuevo Arte de Cocina (1745)

England

The Forme of Cury (1390)

A Proper newe booke of cokerye (1545)

The English Housewife (1615)

The Accomplisht Cook (1660)

The Art of Cookery, Made Plain and Easy (1747)

Part II

What's Past
Is Prologue

A Gargoyle with Three Faces, Not Just Two-Faced (Old French, 15th century, gargouille, meaning "throat")

Chapter 4

A Very, Very Brief History
Of European Cookbooks

The Europeans of the late Middle Ages knew how to eat well. It would be a shame, for us and our taste buds, not to avail ourselves of their experiences.
~ Terence Scully [15]

Before you grab your favorite historic cookbook from your bookshelf or seek out a digital facsimile on the Internet, step back and consider the history of modern publishing.

Modern readers often find it difficult to grasp the importance of the invention of the printing press, with its moveable type. The closest analogy might be the invention of the personal computer. In both cases—printing and computing—vast amounts of knowledge became available to more and more people. With that knowledge came a greater democratization, up to a point. In the case of book buying, as in the acquiring of computers and the accessing of the Internet, the specter of money arose. When scribes were no longer needed to painstakingly copy text onto pages of vellum or parchment, even the poorest person could pay a penny for a broadside or other tract. Provided that he or she could read … . [16]

Before the invention of printing, most culinary manuscripts fell into the category of formularies or books of medical advice, dispensing "receipts" for good health, called *Regimina sanitates*. Many of these works originated in monasteries and convents, copied by scribes. Once cookbook publishing became common after Johannes Gutenberg's invention of moveable-type print-ing around 1438, many of these early manuscripts began to surface in print. But few new cookbooks appeared until after the sixteenth century.

Why not?

People found that the historic cookbooks and cookery manuals worked just fine, allowing them to prepare medicines, luxurious dishes, and preserve food, just as you and other modern cooks turn to Grandma's early copies of *The Joy of Cooking* or *The Fannie Farmer Cookbook*. Religious and medical concerns determined the composition of menus as well. Dishes for fast days abounded. On average, a print run for these early cookbooks numbered a whopping 500 to 2,000 copies. But many cookbooks succumbed to the ravag-es of time, mice, dampness, fire, and mold.

Early cookbooks, at least the survivors, shared many commonalities, not at all surprising considering that copying and borrowing that occurred con-stantly. Plagiarism, no problem! [17]

Humoral Theory—Nothing to Laugh About!

Cookbooks mirror the political and social climates surrounding their authors, in addition to matters of food and cookery and health. Many present-day food combi-nations originated as practices thought to be healthful in medieval or Renaissance times, maintaining bodily balance, thus ensuring smooth functioning of the body and mind. Fish tempered with acid, lemon or vinegar or verjus, comes to mind. "Medicine and cuisine are siblings!" underlay much medicinal thought.[18]

Dating to the days of Hippocrates and Galen, both of whom no doubt influ-enced the tenth-century Persian writer Avicenna, the humoral theory of diet and health prevailed for centuries.[19] Medicinal and culinary practices relied upon a complicated series of rules and interrelationships based on four bodi-ly fluids. Blood, phlegm, yellow bile, and black bile intertwined and dictated what could be eaten or avoided. Adherence to this system slowly waned af-ter Andreas Vesalius published *De Humani Corporis Fabrica* in 1543. By 1628, when William Harvey's *De Motu Cordis* appeared, humoralism receded into the background, remnants of it appearing in some folkloric beliefs and in certain food combinations.

The humoral system followed no logical pattern, at least not by modern scientific standards. Cooks and physicians paid a great deal of attention to states of heat and moisture in the body. They believed that if certain characteristics—or humors—were out of balance, your health suffered. By eating certain foods, or avoiding them, depending upon your inherent nature, wellness and balance could be achieved. In other words, "A good physician must be a good cook."

Complexion, digestion, and fecal elimination concerned the good doctors of the day. By adding certain ingredients, such as hot and dry spices to cold or moist foods, dishes could be brought into balance. And theoretically achieve good health. Platina's *De honesta voluptate et valetudine* (On honest indulgence and good health, 1465) catalogued much of the dietary thinking of the medieval and Renaissance periods.[20]

Good health, you'll learn, preoccupied people then as much as now.

The "doctrine of similarities," for example, suggested that by eating certain foods, a person would imbibe the characteristics of the thing eaten. Think of testicles. That same word applied to female ovaries as well as the male organs. The hoped-for result of eating such food would be increased fertility. Eating the heart of a strong animal would strengthen your weak heart, while goat flesh could make you randy. If you caught too many rabbits, you might take on their fearful nature by eating their meat.

In another aspect of the four humors, the "doctrine of signatures," the diner considered the effect of color or shape or both. Red foods could provide heat when coldness prevailed. Dark red flesh ensured a state of dryness and heat.

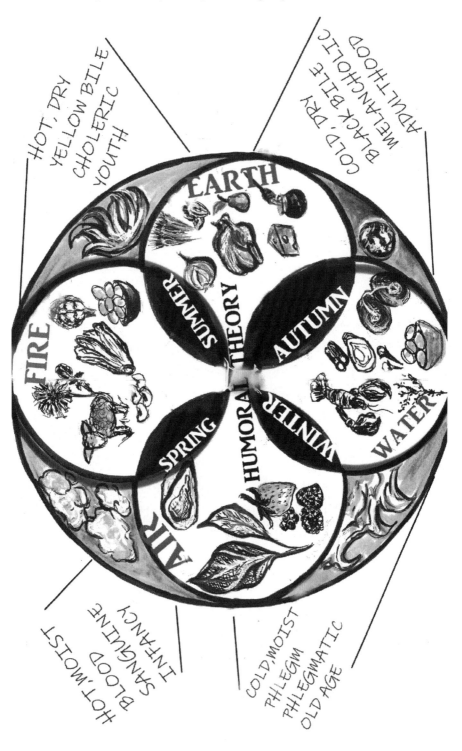

HOT, DRY
YELLOW BILE
CHOLERIC
YOUTH

COLD, DRY
BLACK BILE
MELANCHOLIC
ADULTHOOD

EARTH

SUMMER

THEORY

AUTUMN

FIRE

SPRING

HUMORAL

WINTER

WATER

AIR

HOT, MOIST
BLOOD
SANGUINE
INFANCY

COLD, MOIST
PHLEGM
PHLEGMATIC
OLD AGE

Light-colored meat, such as chicken and other poultry, promised cold and moistness, to tame the heat of a fever or a hot, dry choleric temperament. Eating the ruby-red flesh of swans, for example, might lead you into a melancholic state, or exacerbate an already existing one.

In summary, as Karen Hess states, "Health of the mind and body is the perfect equilibrium among four humors: choleric, hot and dry, characterized by bilious complexion and a fiery temperament; phlegmatic, cold and moist, characterized by a pale complexion and apathy; melancholic, cold and dry, characterized by sullenness and depressed spirits; and sanguine, hot and moist, characterized by a ruddy complexion and great appetites and capacities."[21]

Evolution of the European Cookbook

Three major stages in the historical development of printed cookbooks ensued. Within each stage, discussed below, you'll find many sub-stages and trends pertaining to most Western cultures and parts of the non-Western world, particularly where colonialism held sway.

Any discussion of European culinary history must include the allure of spices. Beginning around 1173 A.D., Venice rose as the chief European trading center for these sought-after ingredients. Its stranglehold on the overland journeys to the East along the Silk Road drove, in part, the race to find a sea route to the East. The Age of Exploration—1400s to 1600s—changed the world far beyond the expectations of the initial players: Portugal, Spain, France, and England. Spices predominated in the recipes of the Late Middle Ages and early Renaissance. However, as their cost decreased, spices became less important to the elites. And cookbooks demonstrated a trend toward using fewer spices.

Cookbook author Anne Willan rendered the history of cookbooks in marvelous graphic form in 2013 when she published "The Cookbook Tree of Life," designed by Keith Cranmer.[22]

By the time a cook, or other personage, recorded recipes on vellum or parchment, you can be sure that such recipes had existed for quite some time, albeit in oral form. Yes, it's possible that some culinary genius woke up one morning and exclaimed, "Today I will add mint to the eel instead of XYZ!" But the role of tradition and beliefs in humoral theories likely made wild innovation a rare act. The constraints of the rigorous fasting demanded by the Roman Catholic Church added another dimension to the history of cooking and menu planning in Europe. This led to the creation of recipes for so-called "fat" and "meagre" kitchens, "flesh" days and "fast" or "fish" days.

Male and Female Authors

Until the nineteenth century, men wrote most of the published cookbooks. A few exceptions existed. Consider Hannah Woolley's *The Queen-Like Closet* (1670). As the pithy Doctor Samuel Johnson quipped, "Women can spin very well, but they cannot write a good book of cookery."[23] Happily, history proved the good doctor wrong.

Male cookbook authors—for example, Bartolomeo Scappi (*Opera dell'arte del cucinare*, 1570)—wrote for *maitres d'hotel* of large, wealthy estates and palaces of kings and queens, powerful noble families, and high-ranking church officials. French authors, such as Guillaume Tirel—also known as Taillevent—and his *Le Viandier* from the 1200s or 1300s influenced culinary trends throughout Europe. Another French manuscript thought to be from 1306, "The Little Treatise," may actually predate Taillevant's work.

Scholars generally suggest that cookbooks served primarily as *aides-mémoires* for these cooks, a sort of archive meant to pass down necessary information concerning ingredients and techniques for opulent banquets, as well as everyday menus and medicinal remedies. However, Sarah Peters Kernan believes that these early manuscript scrolls saw use in the kitchen, too, rebuking Scully and Mennell.[24] At various times, the gentry immersed themselves in the details of the kitchen and food production, getting their hands dirty, as it were.

An anonymous Italian manuscript cookbook dating to the end of the 1400s, *The Neapolitan Recipe Collection* (*Cuoco Napoletano*), contains many opulent banquet menus. This book follows a pattern representative of many culinary books produced by writers of the day. It provides an example of the recipe collections, or "courtly dining guides" for managers of large noble, royal, and ecclesiastical households.

The master/head of the kitchen staff relied on these recipe collections for instructing the household's cooks and their staffs. In the earliest manuscripts, authors failed to mention cooking times, ingredient quantities, and

A Brace of Fowl, or, a Cook's Delight

number of servings. Later, especially with Italian manuscripts emerging in the late fifteenth century, albeit infrequently, some writers occasionally included this information.

Compilers organized these books in various ways, usually by ingredient or part of the meal. A number of early cookbooks focused on the health aspects of foods, including the hot-cold theories and humors stemming from a health manual, the *Tacuinum Sanitatis* of Ibn Butlan of Baghdad, from the eleventh century.

Other authors arranged their works alphabetically by recipe names. They often provided no names for recipes. Much is missing because cooks knew the commonest dishes and procedures so well that no one thought it necessary to mention or record certain details. Take, for example, fruits and vegetables, shown in abundance in paintings of various periods, but often missing in recipe collections. Illustrated cookbooks came into vogue in the 1700s, Bartolomeo Scappi's *Opera* (1570) notwithstanding, a practice that helps culinary scholars in filling in the blanks.

Stage two of cookbook development took the form of household management books intended for housewives and written by both men and women. Rigid and rule-encrusted, the severe tone of these books was often prescriptive and patronizing.

In France, one of the earliest such cookbooks to address women's cooking, *Le Ménagier de Paris*, appeared in manuscript form around 1393. Ostensibly written around 1393 by a wealthy man of a certain age for his fifteen-year-old wife, *Le Ménagier* paints a detailed picture of the daunting tasks necessary to run and maintain an affluent household of the day. Later, Thomas Dawson's *The Good Huswifes Jewell* (1585) focused not only on the desires of the nobility in planning ostentatious banquets, but also on the gentlewomen in charge of day-to-day tasks. French chef Menon's *La cuisiniere bourgeoise* (1746), and *Traite historique et pratique de la cuisine. Ou le cuisinier instruit* (2 vol., 1758) demonstrated other examples of this trend. Martha Bradley addressed the housewife in her six-volume door stopper, *The British Housewife* (1770), as did Isabella Beeton in *The Book of Household Management* (1861). An encyclopedic tome of 1,112 pages, Beeton's masterpiece featured detailed chapters on ingredients and instructions on how to prepare a variety of different dishes. Her book also provided information about medicine, legal terms, menus, and other sundry materials necessary for life at the time.

Later, as female literacy increased, and the Industrial Revolution surged forward, a third stage of cookbook writing emerged. Women put pen to paper. These authors aimed their books at women who managed smaller, less affluent households. Most of these books stressed the importance of economy

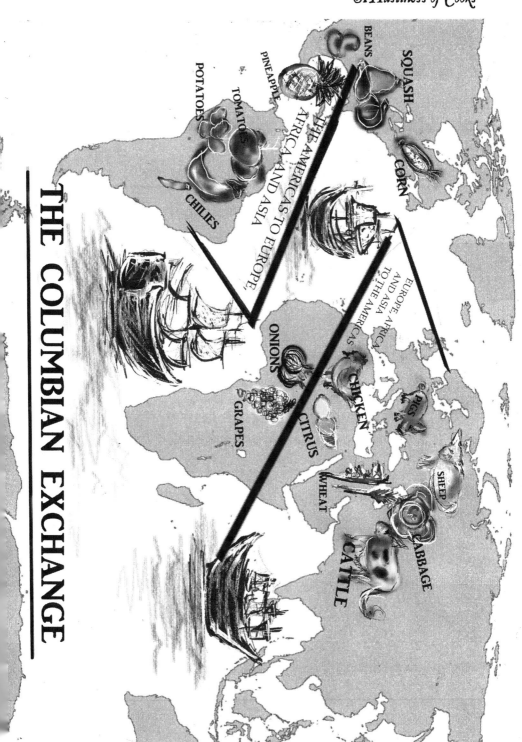

THE COLUMBIAN EXCHANGE

THE AMERICAS TO EUROPE, AFRICA, AND ASIA

EUROPE AND ASIA AND AFRICA TO THE AMERICAS

POTATOES

PINEAPPLE

TOMATOES

CHILIES

BEANS

SQUASH

CORN

ONIONS

GRAPES

CITRUS

CHICKEN

WHEAT

PIGS

SHEEP

CABBAGE

CATTLE

in food preparation. Within this trend you'll find several subgroups of cookbooks: 1) charitable or community, 2) promotional or advertising generated by companies producing food products and kitchen wares, and 3) cooking school/home economics/domestic science movement, focused on health and nutrition topics.

The Age of Exploration

But there's still another aspect of cookbook history to address.

Before any analysis of cookbooks or recreation of recipes takes place, the world-changing events of the Age of Exploration must be considered. Christopher Columbus's voyages to the New World, under the flag of Spain's Catholic Monarchs,[25] opened the door to a vast pantry for people living on both sides of the Atlantic. Earlier voyages undertaken by King Henry of Portugal and his mariners also brought new foodstuffs to untold numbers of cooks. The rigid structure of the humoral system slowed the acceptance of these new ingredients. Where would tomatoes fit into the humoral scheme of things? The influx of ingredients from the New World to the Old—especially sugar—affected cooking on every level. Scholars still debate the impact of this monumental event and refer to it as "The Columbian Exchange."

Thus, cookbooks grew from *aides-mémoires* to instructive works, tapping into their readers' desire to acquire the knowledge and practical skills to replicate the elites' banquets, of "giving readers enough encouragement—as well as literal clarity—so that they would keep on cooking with the text." And buying books.[26]

A Jelly Mold for the Lord's Table

Chapter 5

Historic Cookbooks in England

According to Sarah Peters Kernan, English cookbook production, "… between 1300 and 1600 was remarkably vigorous. England was the most active site of cookbook production in medieval Europe. A higher volume of manuscript cookeries were copied in England than anywhere else on the Continent. English printers initially produced fewer cookbooks than European printers; however, by the late sixteenth century, England was outpacing most of the Continent in the number of different cookbooks produced." [27]

This parade of books rested on the shoulders of what went before. [28] The British Library estimates that fifty handwritten manuscripts still in existence date to the medieval period, which began around the end of the fifth century and lasted until the fifteenth century.

Keep in mind that Scandinavian and Norman French foodways influenced early English cooking, threading through the cooking of the Late Middle Ages, Renaissance, Elizabethan, and Georgian periods.

The Forme of Cury—the first English cookbook according to most authorities—appeared in scroll form around 1390 and led the parade of cookbooks. King Richard II's cooks compiled 200 recipes, several with names influenced by the Saracens, or Arabs, garnered by people returning from the Crusades.

In this book, the listings of ingredients boggles the mind, giving the boot to the idea that cooks of the day produced pottages and nothing else. In the sauces included in the scroll, you see the invisible hand of the Doctoure of Physique, who advised the cooks on how to best balance the humors. Don't be misled by the word "cury," for it means "food," and not the wonderful dishes you might associate with modern India or a curry house in London. The Royal court doled out spices to the kitchen via a section of household called the "spicery," where the Lord Steward watched over the fragrant and highly valuable seasonings crucial for the dishes of the day's menus.

Closely associated with *The Forme of Cury*, you'll find *Utilis Coquinario*, a component of the Sloane manuscript and included in Hieatt and Butler's *Curye on Inglysch* (1985). Thomas Austin's well-known *Two Fifteenth-Century Cookery Books, A Boke of Kokery* (1447), and *A Noble Boke Off Cookry* (possibly 1467) and

others moved toward opulent dishes and the extravagance of elaborate feasts meant to showcase political power during the Renaissance period.

A Noble Boke Off Cookry opens with bills of fare, including one for a sumptuous banquet served to Henry IV. Henry died in 1413, and thus the repast was historical, a snapshot of a much earlier time and of keen interest to those who seek to reproduce dishes of the past. Perhaps the most fascinating description in this book concerns the installation of George Neville as Archbishop of York in 1476. The kitchens required the presence of 62 cooks, who prepared a multitude of dishes ranging from roasted beef to towering confections, or "suttletes" in the shape of castles, animals, and birds.

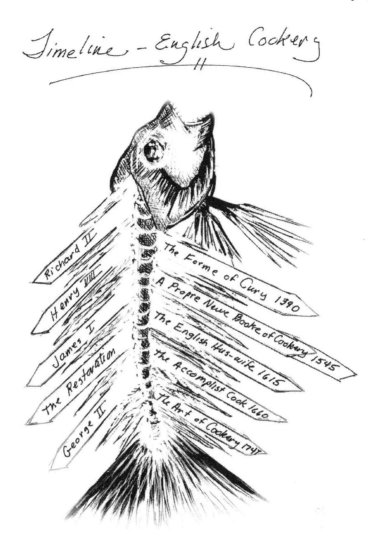

Timeline - English Cookery

Richard II
Henry VIII
James I
The Restoration
George II

The Forme of Cury 1390
A Propre Newe Booke of Cookery 1545
The English Hus-wife 1615
The Accomplist Cook 1660
The Art of Cookery 1747

In 1575, *A Proper Newe Booke of Cookery* reached the public, aimed at female readers. Literacy rates among women tended to be quite low at the time. Therefore, the book fell primarily into the hands of wealthy buyers. The most intriguing thing about this book lies in its adherence to a certain systematic way of recipe writing, including hints about quantities.

Other sixteenth-century cookery books like *A Proper Newe Booke of Cookery* mirrored the opulence generated by the discovery of the New World. Sugar, now accessible thanks to sugar cane grown on plantations in the Indies, figured in all manner of dishes, savory as well as sweet.

A. W.'s *A Booke of Cookrye* from 1591 came next, with details of table service and terse instructions for dishes:

To make white Puddings of the Hogges Liuer.

You must perboile the Liuer, and beate it in a morter, and then straine it with Creame, and put therto six yolks of Egges and the white of two Egs, and grate halfe.

Elinor Fettiplace's 1604 manuscript, rescued from oblivion by Hilary Spurling, still will slow your reading unless you sound out the words as you read.[29] In 1615, Gervase Markham aimed his *The English Hus-wife* at the lady of the manor. Markham's writing reads more like modern English. It doesn't require you to be darting to and from various dictionaries to decipher the text.

Appearing in 1660, Robert May's *The Accomplisht Cook* followed Markham's. May trained in Paris and later cooked under the direction of Arthur Hollinsworth at the Star Chamber in London. Signs of French culinary influences permeate his book. Yet you'll find a plethora of recipes from Italy, Persia, Portugal, Spain, and Turkey, too, signaling the increasing acceptance of "foreign" dishes. The English love-hate relationship with France and her cuisine crops up from time to time in May's work, too. He also included some specific measurements and directions, taking much of the guesswork out of cooking from his recipes.

The Closet Of Sir Kenelm Digby Knight, Opened hit the booksellers' stalls in 1669. It usurped Gervase Markham's *The English Hus-wife*, which sold well in the American colonies and remained a bestseller up until approximately 1683, going into two editions. Digby's use of "closet" in the title plays with the concept of secrecy, of revealing ideas that made aristocratic fare of such mesmerizing interest to those on the outside looking in.

Following Robert May's lead, Hannah Glasse's *The Art of Cookery, Made Plain and Easy* of 1727 made derogatory comments about French cooking. Much of her book originated with *The Whole Duty of a Woman*, published in 1737 by "A Lady."

Martha Bradley's *The British Housewife* has long fascinated readers, with its intriguing detail and precise instructions. Originally printed in a series beginning in 1756, it later appeared as a complete book in two volumes in 1758, totaling a colossal 725 pages. The book—organized by season, with a month-by-month compendium of ingredients—well represents a number of trends ongoing in England at the time. Women authors were becoming mainstream contributors to cuisine, something that did not happen in France until much later. Subtle disdain for French culinary mannerisms was increasing. Women like Martha Bradley could better themselves through cooking. Mrs. Bradley's book never reached the pinnacle of commercial success seen by Elizabeth Raffald's *The Experienced English Housekeeper* (1769) or Hannah Glasse's *The Art of Cookery,*

Made Plain and Easy, and—truth be told—Bradley co-opted many of Glasse's recipes, as was the practice at the time.

The 1700s came to a close with John Farley's *The London Art of Cookery* (1783), Richard Briggs's *The English Art of Cookery* (1788), and Susannah Carter's tome of 1765, *The Frugal Housewife, or, Complete Woman Cook*. Carter's book impacted American cookbooks significantly. Amelia Simmons, author of the first truly American cookbook, aptly named *American Cookery*, relied heavily on Carter's work.

 Still [in spite of other influences such as African and Native American, etc.], the way of our [United States] cooking is English, much as common remains the basis of our law. (Karen Hess, p. 5, *Martha Washington's Booke of Cookery*)[30]

Chapter 6

Historic Cookbooks in Spain

A ll roads lead to Rome. That old adage mostly holds true when it comes to Western cuisine. Any history of cookbooks in the West must begin with the history of Spanish cooking, which in turn evolved from Roman cuisine and rooted itself in early Arab cuisine as well.

You see the impact of Arab cuisine in one thirteenth-century Spanish cookbook that survived the mold and fires of time, *An Anonymous Andalusian*

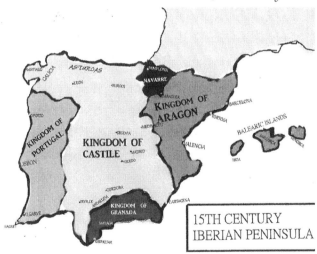

Cookbook.[31] Note that during the medieval period, a number of regions made up what you now think of as Spain or Roman *Hispaniae*: Portugal, Granada, Aragon, Navarre, and Castile.

Written in Catalan in the 1300s, *Libre de Sent Soví* recorded 222 recipes pre-

Timeline — Spanish History

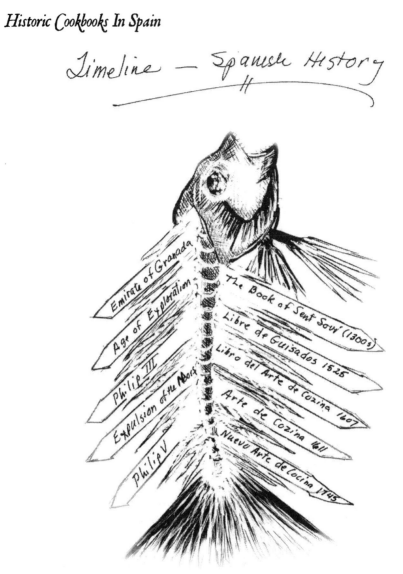

Emirate of Granada

Age of Exploration

The Book of Sent Soví (1300's)

Libre de Guisados 1525

Libro del Arte de Cozina 1607

Philip III

Expulsion of the Moors

Arte de Cozina 1611

Nuevo Arte de Cocina 1745

Philip V

pared in Aragon, long before the influx of foods from the Americas. Other manuscripts dating from this period also demonstrate borrowings from *Sent Soví*, namely *Le livre du cuisinier de l'eveche de Tarragone*, from 1331; and *Com usar de beure e menjar*, by Francesc Eiximenis (1337 – 1409), a cleric who quipped somewhat nationalistically that *"com catalans mengen pus graciosament e ab millor manera que altres nacions,"* or that "Catalans eat more graciously and better than do other nations!"

Another cookbook from the 1300s—*Libre de totes maneres de confits*—included 33 recipes for fruit confits. Its author likely borrowed material from the *Sent Soví* manuscript. The anonymous author of the *Manual de mugeres en el cual se contienen muchas y diversas recetas muy buenas*, from the 1500s, cherry-picked recipes from *Sent Soví*, too.

However, another source of recipes for colonial Spain arrived with the 711 A.D. Islamic invasion of Spain.

These Arab sources, such as the tenth-century *Kitâb al Tabîkh* (The Book of Dishes) by Ibn Sayyer al-Warraq, provide a glimpse of the roots of spicing patterns used in medieval Spanish cuisine and throughout Western Europe. Characteristic ingredients common to Spanish cooking owe much to the presence of Arabs, who dominated the Iberian Peninsula for 800 years, from 711 to 1492. Many of the common flavoring ingredients—cinnamon, nutmeg, sugar—still appear in recipes associated with Spanish and Mexican cooking.[32]

Islam affected Spanish cuisine a great deal. But Roman Catholic convent and monastery cuisine, as well as the innumerable fasting or "fish days," also left their mark on the kitchens of Spain, from palace to hovel. Very likely the daughters of *conversos*—Jews or Muslims or their descendants who converted to Catholicism in Spain and Portugal in the 1300s and 1400s—made significant contributions to the cuisine. These women entered religious life to avoid marriage with Christians. Along with their trunks of clothes, they brought their familial food traditions with them, passing those culinary traditions on to their new communities. In particular, nuts, eggs, sugar, honey, raisins, and frying oil enriched baked goods and other confections. Arab culinary practices likely affected New World cuisine when the Spanish brought Moorish slaves to the New World by Spanish religious orders.[33]

One of the most widely used cookbooks in early modern Spain, Ruperto de Nola's *Libro de guisados, manjares y potajes*, appeared in Castilian in 1525.[34] The original title read as *Llibre del coch* (Book of the Cook), likely written in Catalan or Limousin. As chef to a Neapolitan king Ferdinand (or Ferrando), Nola—also known as Mestre Robert—plucked recipes from many different

regions: Aragon, Provence, Valencia, Italy, and, of course, Catalonia. These recipes formed the basis for many cookbooks that came later. Nola's work straddled the Late Middle Ages and the early Renaissance period. He suggested cooking times, ingredient quantities, and included some detailed instructions. It is not unreasonable to conclude that this style of cookbook writing influenced future works far and wide, which many early innovations tend to do.

Several cookbooks, along with *Libre de Sent Soví*, represent the core of Spanish cookbooks until the nineteenth century. These books included:

- *Libre de totes maneres de confits,* 1300s Catalan

- Enrique de Villena, *Arte cisoria: arte de trinchar o cortar con cuchillo carnes y demás viandas* (1420)

- Domingo Hernández de Maceras, *Libro del Arte de Cozina* (1607)

- Francisco Martínez Montiño, *Arte de cocina, pasteleria, vizcocheria, y conservia* (Art of Cooking, Pastry, Savory Pastry and Preserves, originally printed 1611, reissued 1725 and 1795)

🐕 Diego Granado, *Libra del arte de cocina* (1614)

🐕 Juan de Altamiras, *Nuevo arte de cocina* (1745)

🐕 Juan de la Mata, *Arte de reposteria* (1747)

Of particular interest is Martínez Montiño's book, which boasted one of the first printed recipes for potatoes. As you've seen, the 1611 version of *Arte de cocina, pasteleria, vizcocheria, y conservia* traveled with Don Diego de Vargas, Spanish governor of New Mexico and formed part of his library in Santa Fe, influencing future authors, in particular the anonymous Mexican writer of *La Cocinera Poblana* (1872). The Age of Exploration and the subsequent *Siglo de Oro*, or Golden Age, ushered in a plethora of exotic ingredients for the eager and adventurous aristocrats of Spain. And eventually all of Europe.

A Kitchen without a Mortar and Pestle is a Sorry Place Indeed

Part III

Theories Behind Historic Cookbook Analysis

Chapter 7

Living History: Using Cookbooks in Historical Research

Many writers have explored the use of cookbooks as sources for various types of historical research.[35] Few provide in-depth methodology for carrying out the process. Fewer still have applied such analysis to cookbooks from cultures other than England, Italy, and France.[36]

When you ask the larger historical questions about food and diet, you're going to be looking at four major contexts:

1. The political

2. The physical

3. The social

4. The aesthetic

Dr. Maryellen Spencer pioneered methodology for deciphering cuisine in an historical context. Unfortunately, Spencer died a few months after she received her Ph.D. for her dissertation, "Food in Seventeenth-Century Tidewater Virginia: A Method for Studying Historical Cuisines." Her work presented a clear method for the study of cuisines when written material is mostly non-existent.

Spencer relied on unique primary sources, including the pioneering work of archaeologists Ivor and Audrey Noel Hume, who excavated sites around the original Jamestown settlement and Williamsburg in Virginia. Audrey

Noel Hume's *Food* (1978) provides material of great interest to culinary historians and historical archaeologists. These scholars utilize many different types of documents in their endeavors, but cookbooks are not often thought as go-to sources.

Cookbooks are more than merely lists of recipes and ingredients. Even when no commentaries accompany the recipes, you can recreate the culinary world of people who might have eaten food prepared using the recipes as guidelines. Cookbooks, if you read closely, aid in reconstructing conditions about which other documents or evidence shed little light.

What you learn from examining cookbooks:

- Availability of foodstuffs: varieties, forms, and sensory properties
- Food production methods
- Food choices and preferences
- Physical facilities for food preparation and storage
- Cooks and other kitchen workers
- Servers and other servants
- Food preparation and utensils

- Food storage methods
- Food preservation processes
- Feeding patterns and food habits
- Food style and aesthetics
- Dining: presentation and serving of food
- Culinary heritage and traditions
- Beliefs and values: taboos and religious restrictions
- Ideology of food

Chapter 8

Cookbook Analysis: What is Your Question?

Once you determine what basic questions you want to ask, your search begins for illuminating material. Accomplish this by examining certain characteristics found in cookbooks:

- **Title pages:** Does the title page act as a rich source of information about the author, patrons, and other biographical information?

- **Action words:** Do these illustrate how cooking took place?

- **Equipment and utensils:** What do action words describe or imply? Do you see indications of trade goods or local industries providing materials for these tools?

- **Kitchen organization:** How did cooks operate in the space, and how many people needed to be there to produce the food?

- **Ingredients:** How do ingredients indicate seasonality, rural or urban location? How did people replenish their pantries and other food-storage spaces? How many recipes contain the same ingredients?

- **Procedures and steps:** Again, how many people might the cook need to help prepare the food? What equipment seems to be necessary to carry out these procedures? What is being left out of the text? Why?

- **Textures of foodstuffs and final dishes:** Are there hints as to what people sought or rejected in terms of foodstuffs?

> **Flavors:** What do these suggest in the way of basic cultural markers and trade interactions?

> **Details about serving:** What clues indicate wealth, or the lack of it, as well as other objects of material culture?

> **Appearance of the final dish:** Does the author include illustrations? Does the recipe describe how the dish should appear?

The key here is to focus on each of these points one at a time. Not every cookbook renders up all these aspects. Another problem lies with the vocabulary used during different periods of history. Many historians rely on the *Oxford English Dictionary* when attempting to decipher early English cookbooks such as *The Forme of Cury* (1390). Glossaries and typologies for articles of material culture also assist with the interpretation of the environment and surroundings of the people of the period in question.

See **Chapter 15: Online Tools** and **Selected Bibliographical Resources** at the end of this book for resources for researching your questions.

Chapter 9

How to Begin: Step-by-Step Analysis of Historic Cookbooks

When you're ready to begin recreating recipes from historic cookbooks or analyzing them for what they can contribute to the historical record, it's important to remember that not every cookbook will provide you with the following information. This section simply gives you general suggestions on what to look for as you select recipes and analyze the subtexts of old cookbooks.

There's another thing to keep in mind: Only a limited number of cooking techniques exist, regardless of time period, culture, and aesthetics.

A Word about Authenticity

Forget about authenticity. No matter how hard you try, you'll never achieve true authenticity. To ensure "authenticity" in your recipe reconstructions, you would have to have the same ingredients, grown or raised on the same land, with the same wood or coal for fuel, and cooking utensils used during the time period.

A Word about Sources: The Three "Ts"

A caveat: Lost in translation? In using any cookbook transformed into anything other than the original language, you must take care to be sure of the origin and authority of the authors or editors or translators responsible for the final work. Paleography, the "the study of ancient writing systems and the deciphering and dating of historical manuscripts," assists researchers attempting a transliteration and/or transcription of a document. Furthermore, as Terence Scully states in his introduction to *The Viandier of Taillevent*, if you find multiple versions of a manuscript or book, you must choose one as a baseline. According to Scully, that baseline is most likely to be the earliest one. Why not choose the latest, more complete copy? Because the latest copy may well include a number of changes and additions, reflecting entirely different time periods.

Transliteration

A transliteration refers to a cookbook converted to script that a modern reader can understand. Consider Samuel Pegge's edition of the 1390 *The Forme of Cury*, originally written on a scroll by King Richard II's master cooks. This version includes Old English letters such as "thorn" or Þ ("th") or "u" for "v." Then there's yogh, written as ȝ, a "gh" sound. One of the most frankly annoying problems in reading old printing lies with the use of the long, medial, or descending "S." Looking like a modern "f," this "S" can be confusing.

Other letters and marks that might trip you up include the following:

ȝ = rounded r, also called rotunda

Æ or æ = aesch or ash

‾ or ~ = macron and tilde, used to indicate a missing letter or an abbreviation

You will also likely come across situations where "u" could be "v" and vice versa. Ditto with "i" and "j."

And you have cases where "n" = "u," as in the recipe for "Sawse Blaunche" in *The Forme of Cury*. One of the ingredients listed is "verions." The word "verions" doesn't appear in the *Oxford English Dictionary* or other sources. Why not? If you take the "i" for a "j" and the "n" for a "u," you'll end up with "verjous," which makes sense. Verjuice, or *verjus*, played an important role in many recipes of the time.

Transcription

A transcription concerns a cookbook set in type or a font understandable to the modern reader, without any special or unusual characters. Joan Santanach's version of *The Book of Sent Soví* provides an example of this type of cookbook.

Translation

A translation transforms a work from one language into another. Again, Joan Santanach's version of *The Book of Sent Soví* provides an example of this type of cookbook as well.

Title Pages and Frontispieces

What might you learn from the title page of an historic cookbook?

I beg your indulgence here with this long discourse on title pages. Mrs. Martha Bradley's magnificent opus, *The British Housewife* (1756), has long been one of my favorites. As noted previously, it never achieved the renown awarded to many of her contemporaries.

First of all, take a look at the following illustration. It's the frontispiece from Mrs. Bradley's book. "Frontispiece" hails from the French word *frontispice*, originally an architectural term referring to decorations of the facade of a building. Although frontispieces purportedly show scenes such as this, as with all art and photography, a small grain of salt must be taken, as with a well-salted margarita. Here you see what appears to be a kitchen set up for roasting meat (and catching the drippings), the layout of a hearth for boiling, as well as a work table for making pies and storing tools. The wall above the hearth holds other tools and pot lids, while the far wall stores plates, and the ceiling grate supports the weight of what looks like a ham. Kitchen space speaks of the size of this household, which is not one found in a grand palace. *Docet parva pictura, quod multae scripturae non dicunt.* In other words, perhaps, a picture is worth a thousand words.

But it's the title page, much like that very important first sentence in today's

Frontispiece to Martha Bradley's The British Housewife

definition of good writing—the lede, in other words—that beguiles the reader most and draws her (or him) in.

Mrs. Bradley aimed her book at readers in the country (provinces) as well as London. The cook, the housekeeper, and gardener will find something useful in the book, she suggested, by emphasizing those professions in a larger font. The key word throughout appears to be "Ingredients." She stated that she covers fresh provisions, but the greatest emphasis lies

70

with pickling and preserving. Following that comes the signal that the book provides a guide to getting through the year, seasonality as it were, a "Bill of Fare for each Month." A wide range of dishes is promised, and not costly ones either, foretelling the surge toward economy in the cookbooks of the 1800s, indicating that grand households were not of the greatest concern to the author. She included "Foreign" ingredients, too, implying the increasing commerce and travel of the British as their empire bloomed. She even hinted that illiterate persons will benefit from her book, due to the "curious copper plates" … "by which even those who cannot read will be able to instruct themselves." Finally, in the end, Mrs. Bradley let it be known that she came from Bath, a fashionable place to be indeed, and that she possessed "upwards of Thirty Years Experience." She concluded her advertisement, for that is what it is, with a most telling word: "Practice."

Thus, she sealed the deal by pointing out her street creds, making sure that her platform, brand, niche, whatever rests in the reader knowing of "what is necessary to be done in Providing for, Conducting, and Managing a Family throughout the Year." Mrs. Bradley's contribution to the world of cookery took many tacks, but possibly the greatest of them is this: for the first time a female author wrote for the housewife and not the lady of the manor.

Action words

Words such as "set," "lay," "caste (add)," "strew," "grate," "shred," "boil," "drain," "roll," etc., hint at what you need to do to complete the dish. These words also convey a great deal of meaning behind the cooking techniques implied by action words and the sophistication of the cooks of the time and class level.

Equipment and Utensils

Using the action words that you've picked out of the text, you'll sense what equipment might be necessary, even if recipes don't mention the necessary tools. "Shred" suggests a knife. "Grate" implies some sort of grater. "Boil" indicates a pot. "Drain" means cooks must have some sort of colander or sieve at hand. "Bolting cloth" indicates the need to strain liquids. And so on.

Illustrations rarely appeared in cookery books prior to the 1600s. Guesswork may take front stage in your analysis.

Kitchen Organization

Some cookbooks, particularly those meant for household stewards and *maîtres d'hotel*, provide hints as to what kitchen staff the household required. This can be of use to archaeologists, for example, for it could explain why certain kitchen sites are laid out as they are. If you're recreating recipes for a large quantity of food for a festival, be sure you break down the recipes to determine what staff you might need to carry out specific tasks.

Ingredients and Flavors

As is to be expected, cookbooks provide a window into ingredients usually available to cooks in a certain time and place. Just because cookbooks authors mention these items, it doesn't mean that such things were widely available

and used. Or even eaten. What is true, most likely, is that people knew about ingredients listed in recipes, either through trade, travel, or local conditions. When recreating recipes or planning menus, take care not to include New

World ingredients unknown to Europe, or elsewhere, prior to 1492. (See Appendix 1 for a detailed list of these.)

You might want to consider a few other aspects related to ingredients. These factors could provide you with insight into the culinary culture of the time period:

- List ingredients and tally their percentages in the cookbook. Common ingredients would likely be more readily available.

- Categorize recipes by type. Count how many of each appear in the book. If earlier books included many recipes for game, and game is rarely mentioned in later books, you could surmise that game became scarcer over time. This is the case with the cookbooks written by Gervase Markham and Robert May.

- Chart various characteristics of the books. You may observe trends taking place over decades or centuries.

Procedures and Steps in Food Preparation: Cooking

When you examine whatever recipe(s) you've chosen, you will immediately see patterns in the way you're to prepare various dishes. List the ingredients and the steps in the procedure as the author lays these out, because many recipes tend not to be chronological in their execution, at least not as written. Make a chart or *aide-mémoire* in a form that makes sense to you. This part of the process is, obviously, the crux of the whole matter. Record every step and, if the dish bombs, adjust the ingredients with your next attempt. For reference, refer to modern cookery books such as *The Joy of Cooking* (1964). Jane Grigson's *English Food* (1974) and Claudia Roden's *The Food of Spain* (2011) might also be useful for help visualizing final outcomes for recipes included in later chapters here. Check other sources if you're not 100 percent certain you're making fritters, for example. Your goal is to discover possible similarities between your historic recipe and modern versions, if any.

Remember that although Claude Lévi-Strauss discussed roasting, boiling, and smoking in his classic work, *The Raw and the Cooked*, cooking techniques tend to be quite universal, no matter where or when in the world cooking takes place.

Certain words used in period recipes send signals to you, the modern cook. Recipes from the Late Middles Ages often include the following words:

- wine, almond milk, verjuice, vinegar, meat broths = liquids

- liver, eggs, cheese, bread/crumbs = binders

- pepper, ginger, cinnamon, cloves, *Poudre Douce, Poudre Forte,* rosewater = spices

Cooking Processes and action words: Clues for Recipe recreation

Cutting	Reducing	Incorporation of Substances	Liquid Separation	Dry Separation	Tenderizing	Increase Digestibility
Slice	Puree	Mix	Squeeze	Grind	Ferment	Heat
Chip	Mash	Stir	Press	Mill	Curdle	Dry-bake/ Roast
Dice	Stew	Beat	Skim	Pound	Marinate	Toast
Carve	Boil	Whip	Leach	Grate	Pickle	Moist-steam
Chop	Strain	Blend	Rinse	Shred	Mold	Boil
Mince		Fold			Steam	Fry
					Soak	Smoke
						Grill

Adapted from Rozin, 1982.

In the final analysis, cook the dish so that *you* will want to eat it!

Textures of Foodstuffs and Final Dishes

Note any allusions to texture, for these references indicate what cooks and their audience might have considered delicious. Like the use of spices and herbs, textures play a major role in what people consider edible.

Appearance of the Final Dish and Serving Details

Check modern recipe books if you are uncertain about how your dish might be treated today. But, again, remember that just because cooks named a dish one thing in the past, it doesn't mean that the modern dish is the same thing. Francisco Martínez Montiño's *"Capirotada"* proves this point: his dish resembles an *Olla Podrida* more than it does the modern version, which is a bread pudding festooned with dried fruit and nuts. Examine other cookbooks from the same era to determine how other cooks may have treated the same recipe. Of course, you're bound to run into plagiarism, finding the exact same recipe written verbatim elsewhere!

Monks also Found God Among the Pots and Pans

Chapter 10

Getting Started with Recipe Reconstruction: The Basics

In choosing a recipe for reconstruction, you must first consider the following:

1. Your experience in cooking

2. Ingredients and equipment available to you

3. The occasion for which you're cooking: Madrigal dinners, reenactments at historical sites, dinner parties, or restaurant menus, etc.

4. Your facility with the language used in the original recipe

5. The need to first read and translate the recipe into modern terms, consulting contemporary versions of the same recipe where possible

6. The intricacies of the cooking process

7. Listing and selecting your ingredients

8. Determining what the final product should be. Due to the fluidity of recipe naming in the past, you might find it useful to compile a list of similar recipes—or concordance—before you start recreating your chosen recipes

9. Cooking times and procedures

10. Presentation and serving details

You may find the following form useful as you begin your analysis of your chosen recipes. Modify it according to your needs.

The recipe analyses in Chapters 11 and 12 follow this form:

Step-By-Step Recipe Reconstruction Form

1. Recipe name and source:

2. Original recipe. Check for similar recipes in other sources, if possible. Include translation and transliterations as well.

3. Ingredients in original recipe:

4. Equipment, procedures required, action words

5. Unclear words and language:

6. Resources used to clarify wordage, procedure, other issues:

7. Notes regarding the final dish, what you would redo, change:

8. Modern version of the recipe:

Before You Begin Cooking...

Even before you select your first recipes for recreation, examine your kitchen equipment and your pantry.

To tackle the recipes analyzed here in this book, you'll need most of the following basic equipment:

Knives (the sharper the better!)

Cutting board or other surface for chopping

Grater

🦌 Mortar and pestle

🦌 Strainer or sieve of some sort. (I've found that a *chinois* works best) [37]

🦌 Cast-iron skillet

🦌 Terracotta baker with a lid

🦌 Other baking dishes

🦌 Several different size pots for boiling and stewing

🦌 Jars of spice mixes (See below.)

Poudre Douce/Poudre Fine

3 tablespoons ground ginger

2 tablespoons granulated sugar

1½ tablespoons ground cinnamon

1 teaspoon ground cloves

1 teaspoon ground nutmeg

Mix everything together and store in air-tight container in dark, dry place. NOT above your stove!

Poudre Forte

1½ tablespoons ground ginger

1 tablespoon ground cinnamon

½ teaspoon ground mace

½ teaspoon ground cloves

½ teaspoon fresh ground black pepper

½ teaspoon grains of paradise, ground with a mortar and pestle (optional)

Mix everything together and store in air-tight container in dark, dry place. NOT above your stove!

Poudre Blanche

2 tablespoons granulated sugar

1 teaspoon ground cinnamon

1 teaspoon ground ginger

Mix everything together and store in air-tight container in dark, dry place. NOT above your stove!

Stock your pantry, too:

- Sea salt, fine
- Black peppercorns
- Cinnamon, both sticks and ground
- Ginger, ground
- Cloves, ground
- Coriander, fresh and ground
- Saffron
- Sugar
- Lard
- Olive oil
- Bacon
- Onions
- Garlic
- Parsley, fresh
- Rosewater
- Red-wine vinegar or verjuice, if you can find it
- Almonds
- Raisins

🖤 Bread crumbs, preferably homemade from a solid loaf, not wispy mass-produced bread

🖤 Eggs

🖤 Butter

Keep in mind specific characteristics of the cuisine of the time period you're reconstructing. When you read recipes from medieval and Renaissance sources, you'll find many of the following commonalties:

🐷 Sauces thickened with breadcrumbs or ground nuts[38]

🐷 Flavors enlivened by the addition of tart flavors, such as mustard, vinegar, and verjuice

🐷 Spices (*Poudre Douce, Poudre Fine,* or variations of these)

🐷 Broth

🐷 Fats, usually lard

🐷 Pre-roasted or fried meats, cut up and sauced

🐷 "Sweetening" in the form of honey, sugar, or dried fruits, such as raisins

🐷 Coloring, saffron for example, yellow being the color of warmth and heat

Measurements:

Troy/apothecary weights (medieval)

1 oz = 31.1g

12 oz = 1 pound (373.2g)

Avoirdupois weights (modern American)

1 oz = 28.3g

16 oz = 1 pound (452.8g)

Although the above instructions pertain to the recipes in Part IV, the general idea—choosing equipment and pantry items to fit your preferred historic period—are crucial first steps for recreation of recipes.

There's one more thing to think about.

Once you've decided on your recipe(s), you may need to refer to other cookbooks or sources. Why? These help you to verify—as much as is possible—that you're on the right track as you begin analyzing and preparing your chosen recipe(s).

Some of the following resources represents just a few of the many available. For more, see Chapter 15, "Online Tools" and the **Selected Bibliographical Resources** at the end of this book.

Above all, copies of Michael Ruhlman's books—*Ratio: The Simple Codes Behind the Craft of Everyday Cooking* (2010) and *The Elements of Cooking: Translating the Chef's Craft for Every Kitchen* (2010)—may prove to be some of your most valuable tools as you put your wooden spoon to work.

For English recipes:

- National Trust cookbooks
- Irma Rombauer's *Joy of Cooking*
- Darina Allen's *Forgotten Skills of Cooking: the Time-Honored Ways are the Best – Over 700 Recipes Show You the Way*
- Jane Grigson's *English Food*
- Dorothy Hartley's *Food in England*

For Spanish recipes:

- Coleman Andrews's *Catalan Cuisine*
- Penelope Casas's *The Foods & Wines of Spain*
- Maite Manjón's *The Gastronomy of Spain and Portugal*
- Nawal Nasrallah's *Annals of the Caliphs' Kitchens*
- Claudia Roden's *The Food of Spain* and *A Book of Middle Eastern Food*

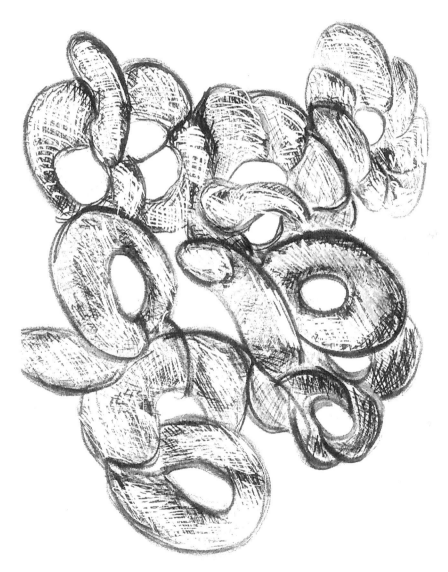

Jumbling Up the Jumbles, What a Perfect Name!

The Eating of Eels,
an Ancient Enchantment

Chapter 11

Using Fire in Recreating Historic Recipes

Maybe you remember cooking with fire as something you did with a sharp stick and a gooey white marshmallow. Maybe you watched your grandfather slap a fish into a hot skillet, sizzling in fat, bathed in the light of one of those Mars-red sunsets in the American Southwest.

There's something magical about fire, isn't there, how it transforms rawness into something edible and bursting with flavor.

From the moment the first spark lit dry wood, and the ensuing fire charred a rabbit's fur or caught a deer in mid-run, humans took to cooking. James Boswell deemed *Homo sapiens* "a cooking animal." Indeed.

According to Richard Wrangham in *Catching Fire: How Cooking Made Us Human* (2009), cooking imparts flavor to the food you eat and jump-starts the digestion process. Your salivary glands awaken, cranking out saliva in anticipation of what's to come. Wrangham pointed out that cooking spared our primate ancestors the need to spend hours chewing food, breaking it down for digestion.

Wrangham also discussed gender-based and historical reasons for women doing the cooking. Historically, knowing how to cook seemed to be a prerequisite for many women entering into marriage. Heaving heavy scalding hot pots, shoveling ashes while dressed in long skirts, and the sheer back-breaking work of the kitchen made this the second most common form of death among women in early America. Keep in mind the need for constant vigilance and awareness while you cook with fire.*

Until the harnessing of coal, electricity, propane, and natural gas, being able to cook meant knowing how to manipulate a wood fire. By 1850 in most of the United States, hearth cooking became old-fashioned, thanks to the invention of the iron stove.[39]

The following discussion focuses on hearth cooking and attempts to summarize what you need to know in order to cook with fire. Some points apply to campfires and three-stone cookery. For more depth on the topic, refer to the chart at the end of this chapter and to the references under "Fire: Cooking with Fire" in the section titled **Selected Bibliographical Resources**.

Of course, any working fire must start with wood. Hardwood works best, because it burns longer and provides more heat. Softwoods—from trees with needles—help to get a fire going. Pine kindling, the resin-rich heart

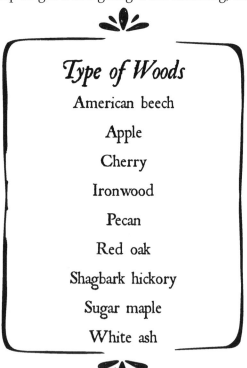

Type of Woods

American beech

Apple

Cherry

Ironwood

Pecan

Red oak

Shagbark hickory

Sugar maple

White ash

of the trees, cut into small eight-to-ten-inch pieces, ignites almost immediately when placed over crumbled-up newspaper. Because of their resinous nature, softwoods impart an undesirable taste to food.

Flames work best for roasting and cooking with a crane. Coals and embers, shoveled into piles on the hearth, act in much the same way as burners on a modern stove. By using cast-iron equipment such as trivets, Dutch ovens, S-hooks, trammels, and ratchets, you regulate the heat you need by 1) raising the cooking utensils up and away from the coals or 2) adding more embers or cooling too-hot spots by covering embers with ash.

Fires must be banked, started several hours prior to cooking. For best results, there should be four to six inches of ash in the fireplace. Word to those who wish to cook in the fireplace: DON'T clean out the ashes! Again, like modern stove burners, the trick is to raise the heat, stabilize it, then reduce the heat. That's precisely how cooking fires work.

A fire undergoes several permutations as it comes to life and then dies down. According to Lennox Hastie[40], those stages are:

Ignition, Smoke, Flame, Embers, Ash, and Cinder

Each of these manifestations demonstrates certain qualities. I've always found it odd that never, at least not in the English language, has there been any coining of words detailing the exact appearance of a fire, allowing the cook to know and name what's happening temperature-wise by eyeballing the coals or embers or ash. After all, English does provide certain precise words and phrases for doneness, such as golden brown, dry in the center, springs back at the touch. And so on. (But "the color of rubies" isn't used in the case of fire!)

You can rely on something called "heat feel" to determine, more or less, what your fire's temperature might be. What does this mean? How long can you hold your hand or foot over the fire and count how long you can keep your hand in place? [41]

Characteristic	Heat Feel	Color
Smoke	20 - 30 seconds	Yellow flame
Hot Flame	5 – 10 seconds	Orange
Hot Embers	1 second or less	Bright orange, nearly white
Medium Embers	3 - 5 seconds	White ash, bright orange embers
Gentle Embers	10 – 15 seconds	Heavy white ash, slowly burning embers
Hot Ash	More than 60 seconds	White gray ash

Chart adapted and summarized from Lennox Hastie, Finding Fire, p. 43.

As a rule of thumb, these characteristics of fire depend upon a number of external factors, including the type of wood you're using, the availability of oxygen to keep the fire going, and your level of pain tolerance. Just to give you an idea of the amount of heat you're dealing with, you'll be floating your tender flesh over 2190 - 2910°F with the Hot Embers above!

Basic Composition of a Fire

Boiling and simmering were perhaps the most common methods of cooking in European cuisine. In *The Magic of Fire*, William Rubel suggests using a tripod with the pot set four-to-six inches away from the fire. As the liquid

begins to simmer, you shove embers under the bottom of the pot, with some piled up against the edges as well.

As for equipment, you'll find a Dutch oven to be most versatile, particularly one with three legs, its own built-in tripod as it were. Hearth-cooking expert Nancy Carter Crump states that if you're a serious hearth cook, you should acquire two Dutch ovens, each capable of handling 1.5 gallons.[42] The flat lids of these ovens allow you to place hot coals on top of the oven, as well as under and around them. By doing this, with the pots nestled among embers and ash, you'll bake bread, biscuits, cakes casseroles, pies, as well as simmer stews and soups and pottages.

Cooking with fire transports you back to the primeval, the visceral.

Have on hand a bucket of water, blankets or other such to smother flames, a fire extinguisher. Wear natural-fiber clothing.

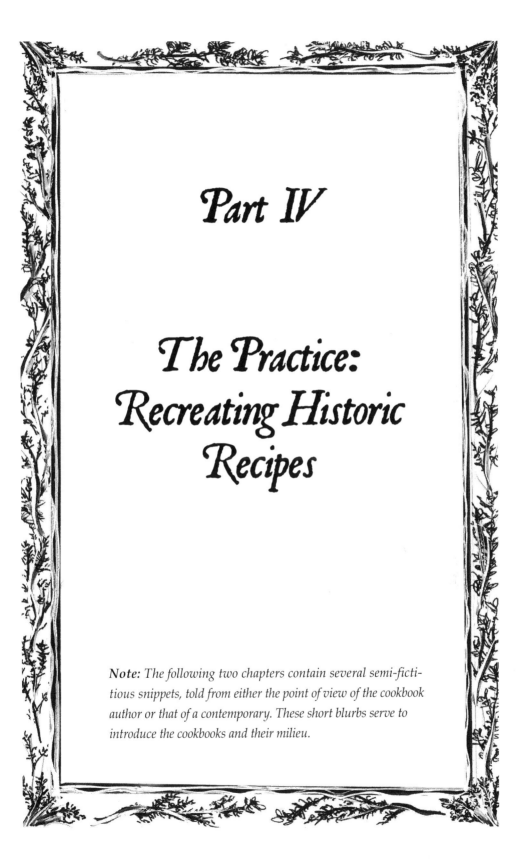

Part IV

The Practice: Recreating Historic Recipes

Note: *The following two chapters contain several semi-ficti-tious snippets, told from either the point of view of the cookbook author or that of a contemporary. These short blurbs serve to introduce the cookbooks and their milieu.*

Medieval Cooks Tasting the Broth

Chapter 12

Step-by-Step Analysis: Spanish Cookbooks

O ne day, autumn's bright oranges and yellows veiling the apple orchard, I found myself in the monastery library, in the company of the chief scribe. Normally, I would never be allowed there. I, a humble cook, although a monk, lack the intricate skills of the scribe, though I make up for it with the wooden spoon and the knife.

My brother monk pulled out several rolls of vellum. Then he gestured for me to approach the worn oak table, stained by the iron-gall ink used for writing. I stared as he unrolled scroll after scroll. I thanked God for bringing me to the monastery at age four, blessing me with the gift of reading and writing Latin and some of the vulgar tongues of the travelers who sat at the refectory table and relished my cooking. Before me lay such riches that I wondered if the Devil himself were about, for the temptation to grab the scrolls and stash them in my mean little cell overcame me. I reached out to touch, but Brother Jacob handed me a stylus and some ink. Motioning for me to sit, he spread out more vellum and encouraged me to write what I saw.

So I did. I copied nearly 100 receipts for everything, from *sofregit* to *Cabrit en Ast*, roast kid and the "spoon dishes" that sustained both the healthy and the sick. My mouth watered as I copied it all, day after day, until the snows began on the eve of All Souls.

Eggplant. Chickpeas. Goat. Pine nuts. Semolina. Octopus. Fish. Chicken. Beef. Pork, of course. Saffron. Cloves. Ginger. Cinnamon, all the strong spices. Such glorious tastes. In my lowly position, I serve the nobles and gentry on pilgrimages, those coming from Italy and further beyond. They tell me tales of their kitchens, of the flavors that emerge, placed before them by servants too numerous to count.

Sent Soví

Step 1: **Recipe Name and Source: Si Vols Fer Escabetx (If You Wish to Make Escabeche), from Sent Soví (14ᵗʰ century)**

Step 2: **Original Recipe and Translation:**

Si Vols Fer Escabetx

Si vols fer escabetx a peix frit, hages brou de peix, mit-hi cebes e oli e sal e juivert, e courà en una olla. Hages llet d'ametlles ab lo brou. Enaprés hages del peix frit –e de cui ten aigua, si n'has—e pic'l ab pa torrat e mullat ab vinagre; e si has pinyons, pica-ne. E mit-hoa bullir en una olla ab bones espècies e agror e dolçor. Aprés hages cebes rodones prim tallades, que hagen quatre dits de llong, e mit-les a sosengar ab oli que a penes bulla. E puis, quan la ceba serà assosengada, que un poc crusca, mit-la ab la salsa quan bullirà, e de l'oli sosengat, de guisa que no hi parega massa; e assorbora-ho de dolçor e d'agror e de sal e salsa. E pots-hi metre panses picadas ab vi o ab vinagre, e posar sobre lo peix frit calent. E deu ésser refredat ans que sia donat.

Jo he vist que hi picaven, ab la salsa, ametlles e avellanes torradas e pa torrat en vinagre mullat, e que en destrempaven ab vi ab vinagre.

Translation of Recipe

If you want to make fried fish in vinegar sauce, make fish broth, put in onions and oil and salt and parsley, and cook all in a pot. Make almond milk with the broth. Then make fried fish—and fish cooked in water if you have any—and mince it with toasted bread moistened with vinegar; and if you have pine nuts, chop them. Put the pot to boil with good spices and verjuice and sweetening. After take round onions about four fingers long, cut them thin, and put them to fry in almost-boiling oil. Then, when the onion is fried, a little crunchy, put it with the sauce when it comes to a boil, and some of the oil from frying, so that it is not too thick; and season it with sweetening and verjuice and salt and spices. And put in raisins soaked in wine or vinegar, and put it on top of the hot fried fish. It ought to be cooled before serving.

I have seen ground almonds or hazelnuts and toasted bread moistened in vinegar, and also infused with wine and vinegar.

Step 3. Ingredients in original recipe:

- 🧄 Fish
- 🧄 Oil
- 🧄 Verjuice and vinegar
- 🧄 Salt
- 🧄 Onion
- 🧄 Parsley
- 🧄 Bread
- 🧄 Pine nuts
- 🧄 "Good spices"
- 🧄 "Sweetening"
- 🧄 Raisins

Step 4. Equipment, procedures required, action words:

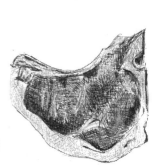

- 🫘 Pots
- 🫘 Knives
- 🫘 Strainer or sieve
- 🫘 Baking dish
- 🫘 Soak/Strain/Grind/Squeeze (implied in making almond milk)
- 🫘 Frying
- 🫘 Boiling

Step 5. Unclear words and language:

- 🐇 The chronology of the recipe doesn't make sense by modern standards.
- 🐇 This seemingly simple recipe hides a lot of preparations: broth, almond milk, fried fish.

🐇 Onions "four fingers long" presented an issue. Would any onions do?

🐇 What species of fish would work best?

🐇 What type of oil?

🐇 What does "good spices" mean?

🐇 Could "sweetening" refer to honey?

🐇 Escabeche is a modern preparation in Spanish cooking. But is it the same thing as this ancient Catalan recipe?

🐇 Exactly where did the manuscript come from? Would knowing that provide clues as to the possible type of fish?

Step 6. Resources used to clarify wordage, procedure, other issues:

🐖 *Sent Soví*, compiled from previous (and unknown) written and oral sources, represents the work of more than one author. It served as an *aide-mémoire*.

🐖 Penelope Casas, on page 239, presents a similar recipe— *"Besugo con Piñones."* Hake?

🐖 The Arab word for oil is *al-zat*, close to *aceite*, Spanish for oil. Olive oil, produced by the Romans, was likely available.

🐖 The dish may be related to Persian preparations. Fish *sikbāj* comes to mind. See Lilia Zaouali's *Medieval Cuisine of the Islamic World* (2009).

Step 7. Notes regarding the final dish, what you would redo, change:

Thicker pieces of fish work better, because the flesh stays moister.

Step 8. **Modern version of the recipe:**

Fish Broth

1½ cups water

¼   pound cod in one piece

2   garlic cloves, peeled and left whole

1   quarter of a medium onion, sliced

¼   teaspoon fine sea salt

2   tablespoons chopped parsley

1   tablespoon olive oil

Place all ingredients in a pot and simmer for 30 minutes.

Almond Milk

1½ cups fish broth

½ cup almond meal or 1 cup blanched almonds, soaked in water and drained

Mix the broth and meal together, let sit, and drain. Alternatively, you could whirl the almonds with the broth in a blender and drain.

Sauce

2   tablespoons olive oil

½   cup onion, sliced thin

½   cup dry bread crumbs, soaked in ¼ cup red wine vinegar

3   tablespoons pine nuts, chopped

1/8 teaspoon each ground black pepper, ginger, cinnamon, cloves

1   teaspoon granulated sugar

½   teaspoon fine sea salt or to taste

1½ cups almond milk

2   tablespoons red wine vinegar

3 tablespoons raisins, soaked in hot water for 30 minutes

In a skillet over medium heat, fry onions in olive oil until crisp. Remove from pan and set aside. Toss the bread crumbs into the hot oil in the skillet, stir until coated with the oil, add the pine nuts. Sauté a couple of minutes until bread crumbs start to turn golden. Add the spices, sugar, and salt. Stir in the almond milk slowly to keep it from splashing as it meets the hot pan. Stir. Sauce will thicken. Use a few tablespoons of water to thin it to a consistency you prefer. Stir in the 2 tablespoons of red wine vinegar. Set aside to cool.

Fried Fish

1   cup all-purpose flour

½   teaspoon fine sea salt

1/8 teaspoon ground black pepper

1   pound cod, or fish of your choice, cut into serving pieces

1   cup olive oil, for frying

Mix flour with salt and pepper on a large plate. Heat the oil until almost smoking. Dredge the fish in the flour until completely coated with flour. Carefully place fish in the oil and fry over medium-high heat until golden brown on both sides. Meanwhile, put some sauce on plates, position fish on top of sauce, sprinkle with the raisins and crisp onions.

Serves 4.

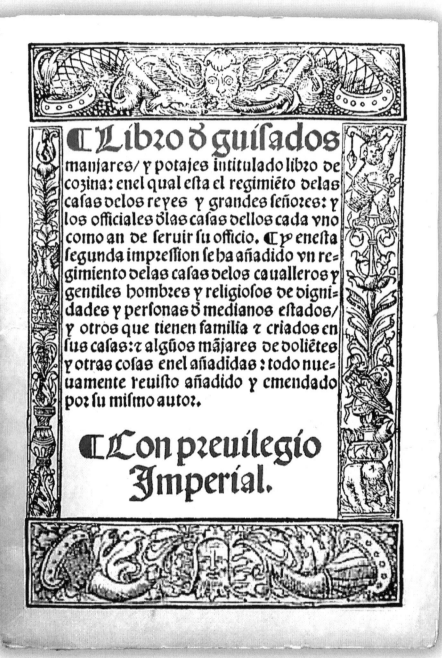

℃Libro d guiſados

manjares/ y potajes intitulado libro de
cozina: enel qual eſta el regimiéto delas
caſas delos reyes y grandes ſeñores: y
los officiales dlas caſas dellos cada yno
como an de ſeruir ſu officio. ℃y eneſta
ſegunda impreſſion ſe ha añadido yn re=
gimiento delas caſas delos caualleros y
gentiles hombres y religioſos de digni=
dades y perſonas ð medianos eſtados/
y otros que tienen familia z criados en
ſus caſas:z algũos mãjares de doliêtes
y otras coſas enel añadidas : todo nue=
uamente reuiſto añadido y emendado
poz ſu miſmo autoz.

℃Con pzeuilegio
Impeꝛial.

Ruperto de Nola
Libro de Guisados

Although I spent time working in the kitchens of Ferdinand, King of Naples, Catalonia—where dark green mountains meet the blue of the sea—formed my character. As well as my cooking.

In Naples, I walked through the markets, my eyes assaulted by the vibrant colors of vegetables, the flow of the cloth covering the bodies of seamen from every port of the *Nostrum Mare*, the aroma of simmering pots of cooks from lands far from where I stood. Their stews and their meats thrilled me and some days I'd rush back to my kitchen, trying to recreate their simple instructions into something far grander for the King's table. In Aragon, in the years surrounding 1480, I cooked in the palace kitchens during the long days and wrote my cookery book in the late evenings, flickering candles casting long shadows over my words.

My book first appeared in Catalan, as *Llibre del coch*, in 1520. By 1525, booksellers could offer their customers a Spanish version, *Libro de Guisados*, printed by Pérez Dávila. Many customers came from the ranks of churchmen, eager, I believe, to prove their worldliness at the table. Their cooks could draw on my 243 receipts to prove their prowess and skill at the hearth. I included many Jewish and Moorish recipes, for their richness must not be lost. To measure how long it would take to cook a dish, I included the adage of prayer, instructing them to say so many "Our Father" or "Hail Marys" to ensure doneness. I learned, over many years of travail, that the kitchen must run like a well-trained fighting force. So, I included a section in my book telling master cooks how to manage eleven different kitchen positions. I confess I found much inspiration in another Catalan cookery book, *Sent Soví*, just as many other cooks find my book to be just as inspiring.

Step 1. **Recipe Name and Source:**

Berejenas ala Morisca **(Eggplants/Aubergines Moorish Style), from Ruperto de Nola,** *Libro de Guisados* **(1525)**

Step 2. **Original Recipe and Translation:**

Transcription of Original Recipe

Mondar las berengenas: y bazarlos quartro quartos: y mondadas dela corteza ponlas a cozer: y desquesean bien cozidas: quitarlas as del fuego: y entonces espremirlas entre dos tajaderos de palo que no les quede agua. Y despues picarlas con un cuchillo. Y vayan a la olla y sean muy bien soffreydas con buen tocino/o con azyete que sea dulce porque los moros no comen tocino. y desque sean bien soffreydas ponlas a cozer en una olla. y echarle buen caldo gruesso: y las grassa dela carne. y queso rallado que sea fino. Y a todas culantro molido. y despues tornearlos con un haravillo como calabaças. y desde sean cercas de cozidas poz unas yemas de buenos batidos con agraz como si fueren calabaças.

Translation of Original Recipe

Peel eggplants and cut them into quarters, and when peeled, set them to cook: and when they are well-cooked, remove them from the fire, and then squeeze them between two wooden chopping blocks, so no water remains: and then chop them with a knife: and send them to the pot and fry them very well, with good bacon or with sweet oil, because the Moors do not eat bacon. And when they are gently fried, put them to cook in a pot and throw in good fat broth, and meat fat, and finely grated cheese, and above all, ground coriander; and then stir it with a *haravillo* like gourds; and when they are almost cooked, put in egg yolks beaten with verjuice, as if they were gourds.

Step 3. Ingredients in original recipe:

- Eggplant/Aubergine
- Bacon
- Eggs
- Meat broth
- Coriander
- Verjuice
- Cheese

Step 4. Equipment, procedures required, action words:

- Roasting fire
- Skillet or other pan for frying
- Knife
- Masher
- Grater?

Step 5. Unclear words and language:

1. Gourds: what does this mean?

2. What's the final dish supposed to look like?

3. Coriander: fresh too?

4. How much broth?

5. No salt?

6. *Haravillo*: what is this?

7. Verjuice: use vinegar instead?

8. Cooking time?

9. Some of the letters in the original recipe, aside from the use of the long "s" in "despues" and "sean," initially seemed confusing. : r

Step 6. **Resources used to clarify wordage, procedure, other issues:**

Gourds: bottle-neck gourds; I sought to clarify their nature, ended up with references to *Lagenaria sicereia*, used in the Old World, related to Italian *cucuzza*, after checking with Clifford Wright's *Mediterranean Vegetables* via Google Books.

After looking in several sources from the period, mostly Italian, I compared this recipe to one in *Sent Soví*, which contains four recipes for aubergines:

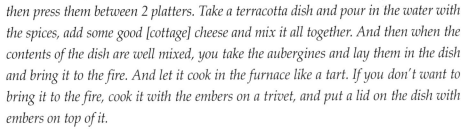

Capitol CLI. Qui parla con se deuen coura albergines en casola

You take the aubergines and peel them and then cook them. And when they are cooked, soak them in the cold water and then press them between 2 platters. Take a terracotta dish and pour in the water with the spices, add some good [cottage] cheese and mix it all together. And then when the contents of the dish are well mixed, you take the aubergines and lay them in the dish and bring it to the fire. And let it cook in the furnace like a tart. If you don't want to bring it to the fire, cook it with the embers on a trivet, and put a lid on the dish with embers on top of it.

Coriander: The recipe refers to ground coriander, because of seasonality. You could use fresh, however, as I did.

Broth: I used two ladles of ham broth which I had on hand from another dish.

Salt: I did not add it, because of the saltiness of the bacon and the ham broth.

Haravillo: I determined this either referred to an implement similar to a masher of some sort OR some sort of stirring device, maybe even something that looks like the implement used to whip hot chocolate drinks.

Verjuice: I decided on cider vinegar as a substitute. According to Mr. Webster, verjuice is "a sour juice obtained from crab apples, unripe grapes, or other fruit, used in cooking and formerly in medicine." [43]

Cooking time: about 30 minutes to roast eggplant. Plus about 25 minutes to finish.

Step 7. **Notes regarding the final dish, what you would redo, change:**

The dish is not attractive by modern standards. You do not want the dish to be too liquid. That's also why I added the crumbled bacon, to boost the eye appeal.

You could make this into a vegetarian dish, using vegetable broth and just add the greenery as decoration.

The final results resemble scrambled eggs, browned a bit by the flecks of eggplant. Use larger eggplants and leave them in chunks.

Step 8. **Modern version of recipe:**

3	Japanese eggplants, roasted at 400°F for 30 minutes, skin on*
2	slices bacon
2	cups fat-rich meat broth
3	egg yolks, beaten
½	teaspoon cider vinegar or verjuice
1/8	teaspoon ground coriander
1	tablespoon parsley or cilantro, minced
1¼	cups grated Havarti cheese, or cheese of your choice

Peel eggplants and scrape out the flesh. Chop the flesh until it almost resembles a puree. You will end up with about 1½ cups.

Cook bacon in medium-size skillet until fat renders out and bacon is crisp. Remove bacon from skillet and drain on paper towels. Crumble bacon for later use. Over medium-high heat, cook the eggplant until it is almost crisp, about 15–20 minutes. Pour in the meat stock—you may have to add more if too much boils off at first. Add the vinegar or verjuice to the egg yolks and pour onto the meat broth and eggplant. Stir until thick. Cook until eggs set, no more than 3–5 minutes.

Add coriander, parsley/cilantro, and cheese.

Transfer mixture to a terracotta serving dish and garnish with the crumbled bacon.

Serves 4.

*Note: These eggplants are long and slender, about 2 inches in diameter at the most. Whatever type you choose, look for smooth firm peel, not wrinkly.

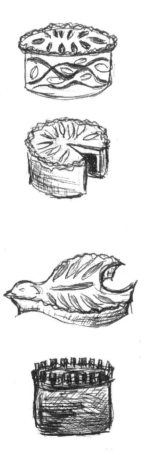

*Pies and Coffins Filled All Manner of
with Scrumptious Victuals*

LIBRO
DEL ARTE DE COZINA:
en el qual se contiene el modo de guisar de co
mer en qualquier tiempo, ansi de carne , como de
pescado, ansi de pasteles, tortas, y salsas, como
de conseruas, y de principios, y postres, a la
vsança Española de nuestro tiempo.

Compuesto por Dominga Hernandez de Maceras,
cozinero en el Collegio mayor de Ouiedo de
la ciudad de Salamanca.

A Don Pedro Gonçalez de Azeuedo Obispo de
Plasencia, del Consejo de su Magestad, &c.

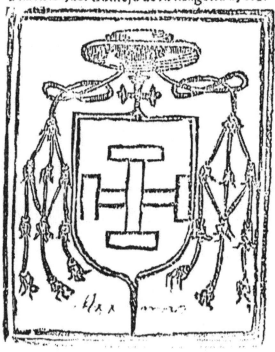

Domingo Hernández Maceras
Libro del Arte de Cozina

Don Domingo never told me where he began his life. He didn't know
the year, either. When I met him, I was studying to become a priest
at the Colegio Mayor de San Salvador de Oviedo of the University
of Salamanca. He would run through the arched cloisters, his black
robes flying in the winter wind, carrying a lamb sometimes, always
the master cook, always intent on food for the churchmen who journeyed far and wide to dine at the abbot's table. There Don Domingo
toiled for thirty years in the kitchen. I came across a copy of his small
cookery book, in the autumn of 1607, just after it had been published.
In it, I counted more than 175 recipes, including many with allusions
to Moorish cooking, such as *Bollo de Clavonia*, of which Don Domingo
said may be called *Bollos Maymones*. He even included detailed directions on how to make English Empanadas with Truffles! Despite his
intention that the book be used in university refectories, it soon found
far wider use. When I arrived in Valladolid to take up my tasks as a
young priest, I carried with me a copy of Don Domingo's *Libro del arte
del Cozina*. It became a great favorite of the nuns who cooked for all
of us priests, for it recalled to them the grand dinners in the houses
of their noble fathers, before the women entered the convent. It came
to pass that these nuns appreciated Don Domingo's work, for despite
the initial inexperience of the novices, his book assisted them in their
learning of the things of the kitchen. The seasons, too,
figured highly in the book. In closing, I must mention
that Don Domingo relied heavily on the work of Señor
Ruperto de Nola for the information about the carving
of meat and birds.

Step 1. Recipe name and source: *De Pollos Rellenos (Stuffed Chickens), Libro del Arte de Cozina* **(1607)**

Step 2. Original recipe, transcription, and translation:

Transcription

Hanse de pelar los pollos, de marcra que no se dessuellen, y les quitaran los papos, de manera que no se rompa el cuero de encima del papo, y se le hara la avertura pequeña por donde se les sacaran las tripas, para que se puede coser, y se picara un poco de carnero de la pierna muy bien picado, con un poco de tocino gordo: perexil, y yerba buena, y unos piñones, y especias, y sal, y huevos que tengan buena sazon, y se rellenara el pollo: tambien se puede rellenar por entre cuero, y carne, como por dedentro, y se le ha de coser la abertura por donde se relleno, por que no se le salga el relleno: y luego le assaran, o cozeran como el señor gustare: y se daran con agraz, o naranja.

Translation

Pluck the chickens, making sure not to tear the skin, remove the craws in such a way as to not break the skin, and make a small opening to take out the guts, so that you can sew the opening, and chop a little of the leg meat fine, with a little fat bacon: parsley, and yerba buena, and pine nuts, and spices, and salt, and eggs with a good flavor, and stuff the chicken: also you may stuff it between the skin and the flesh, as well as inside, and sew the opening where the stuffing is, so that the stuffing doesn't come out; and then roast it, or cook it as the lord and master likes it; and give it verjuice or orange.

Step 3. **Ingredients in original recipe:**

- Chicken—whole
- Ham (see Step 5)
- Bacon
- Parsley
- Yerba buena
- Pine nuts
- Spices
- Salt
- Eggs
- Verjuice/Orange juice

Step 4. **Equipment, procedures required, action words:**

Trussing chicken: requiring needle/thread or string or twine (or something similar, perhaps small strips of wood to use as skewers)

Plucking: implies large pot for softening pin feathers or a fire for singeing feathers

- Chopping
- Stuffing
- Mixing
- Cutting surface
- Knives

🦌 Bowls

🦌 Baking dish or spit

🦌 Spoon

Step 5. **Unclear words and language:**

Pierna in the original, or leg meat, could be confusing. *Pierna* here refers to *pierna de cerdo* or a form of cured pork or ham. Although the recipe requires the use of a pork product, this recipe manifests signs of Persian and/or Arab origins. Many recipes from this time period included ham in various stuffings or "farces."

The original recipe includes several scribal abbreviations: q, o, and e, topped with tildes (~). These represent, respectively, *"que," "on,"* as in *"sazon,"* and *"en,"* as in *"tenga."*

Step 6. **Resources used to clarify wordage, procedure, other issues:**

"Capon Dressing" in Maestro Martino's *The Art of Cookery* resembles this dish.

Step 7. **Notes regarding the final dish, what you would redo, change:**

Adding more eggs binds the stuffing better. Chopping the ham into an almost-pâté-like consistency makes it easier to push the stuffing under the skin and reduces the risk of tearing the skin as well.

Step 8. **Modern version of the recipe:**

1	chicken, approximately 2½ pounds, skin on
2	tablespoons lard, divided
4	slices center-cut bacon, minced fine
¾	pound lean cured ham, minced fine
3	heaping tablespoons pine nuts
½	cup minced fresh parsley
½	teaspoon mint flakes
¼	teaspoon white pepper

¼   teaspoon black pepper

¼   teaspoon ground cinnamon

¼   teaspoon ground ginger

¼   teaspoon saffron

2   eggs, beaten

Plus: 1/8 teaspoon each of white pepper, black pepper, ginger, cinnamon for sprinkling on top of the chicken before baking

Set the oven to 400°F.

Prepare your baking dish by greasing the bottom and up the sides with 1 tablespoon of the lard. Set dish aside. Take the chicken and put it on a clean work surface. In a large mixing bowl, mix together the bacon, ham, pine nuts, parsley, mint flakes, white and black pepper, cinnamon, and ginger. Stir the saffron into the beaten eggs and add to the mixture in the bowl. Shove the stuffing into the body cavity of the chicken and into the neck cavity. Gently push your fingers under the skin of the breast and down to the thighs and place some of the stuffing under the skin as far as you can go. Try not to rip the skin. Truss the chicken with kitchen string or use short bamboo skewers to hold the skin flaps in place over the openings where you've placed the stuffing. Truss the legs with string, too, or use a skewer inserted through both legs to hold them in place. Rub the remaining 1 tablespoon of lard over the chicken and sprinkle with the spice mix. Bake for 2 hours, or until a thermometer registers 165°F.

Note: The bacon and the ham provide enough salt for the stuffing, also called forcemeat. If you prefer your food saltier, by all means add some.

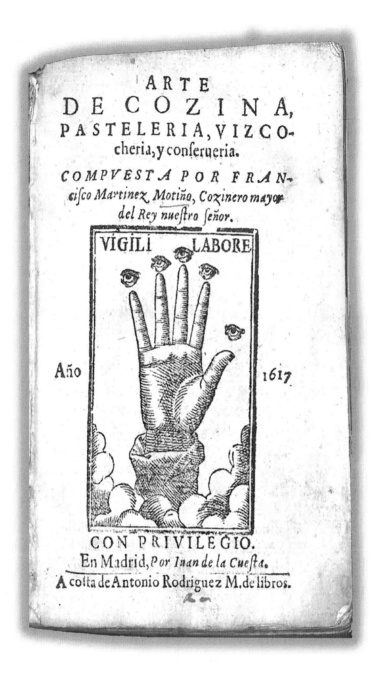

ARTE
DE COZINA,
PASTELERIA, VIZCO-
cheria, y conserueria.

COMPVESTA POR FRAN-
cisco Martinez Motiño, Cozinero mayor
del Rey nuestro señor.

VIGILI   LABORE

Año   1617

CON PRIVILEGIO.
En Madrid, Por Iuan de la Cuesta.
A cofta de Antonio Rodriguez M. de libros.

Francisco Martínez Montiño
Arte de cocina, pasteleria, vizcocheria, y conservia

My earliest memory overcomes me whenever I'm stirring a sweet sauce or plucking feathers from a dead, limp hen. Rain fell that day, hard and cold, my father's beard sparkled with the al-most-frozen drops. I remember my mother's tears, mixing with the rain, so I couldn't tell the difference between the two. I never saw my mother again, for she died on San Juan's day that year. My baby sister lived, but my father turned his face away in his grief. Famine scourged my village in Galicia, and soon tiny Isabella passed into the next world, too.

The coachman leaned down and grabbed my arm, yanking me up so hard I feared he'd wrenched my arm from my shoulder. I bit my lip until I could taste blood. Little did I know I'd be tasting much blood in the years I slaved away in the palace kitchens as a *galopin*, kitchen boy, first in the scullery cleaning the endless pots and pans, licking plates with scraps of food left by the courtiers, my hunger great despite the abundance surrounding me, day in and day out. Then I sat for hours turning great haunches of beef and mutton on spits. All the while, I watched everything the head cook did, thanking God that my mother taught me to read and write, the gift of her sister, a nun in the convent of Santa Maria de la Concepción.

Those words of my youth, and the favor of a head cook in the palace, elevated me to the head cook position when I reached but 20 years of age. In 1585, I began cooking for his royal majesty Philip III, and Philip II's sister, Doña Juana, for a time, in Portugal. The king soon came to want food prepared only by my hand, and I accompanied him on all his journeys throughout Castile and beyond. All in all, I worked in kitchens for over 34 years. Finally, in 1611, I had the great honor of seeing my book of cook-ery appear in print. With *Arte de cocina, pasteleria, vizco-cheria, y conservia*, I summed up my life's work in 502 recipes. My book far surpassed that tiny tome of Domingo Hernandez de Maceras's, *Libro del Arte de Cozina*, for I told how the kitchen must be kept clean and what equipment the cooks must use if they wished their feasts to be successful, admired by the finicky courtiers. And by the king himself!

The good lord in heaven blessed me in those kitchens, for I could lay my hands on every foodstuff in the known world. Or it seemed to be true. Rice, artichokes, spinach, almonds, garbanzos, pomegranates, lemons, oranges. But the meat! Beef and lamb so tender the flesh would nearly melt like ice in your mouth. I even cooked potatoes, those New World oddities I call "testicles of the earth." My 448 recipes paid tribute to the Moriscos, expelled from Spain by my lord Philip III in 1610. I owed my knowledge of pickling, of making *Escabeche de atún* and others, such as *Escabeche de besugo*, to those people.

You would think with all the glorious lords and ladies surrounding me that I would find myself at a place in life in 1629 where ease and comfort would be my lot. Alas, that never came to pass. I sit here, pen in hand, beseeching the new king, Philip IV, to find a place for my two sons in the Alcázar. But I cannot be certain of that.

Step 1. **Recipe name and source:** *Capirotada*, from *Arte de cocina, pasteleria, vizcocheria, y conservia* **(1611)**

Step 2. **Original recipe and translation:**

Transcription

Tomaras lomo de puerco, y salchichas, perdizes todo asado, y haras torrijas de pan, y iras armando tu sopa con torrijas y solomo, y salchichas, y perdrizes : han de ser hechos quartos las perdizes, y el solomo hecho pedaços : e iras poniendo todo este recaudo en lechos y como fueras echando las torrijas, y la carne, iras

Sopa de Capirotada.

TOmaras lomo de puerco, y salchichas, y perdizes todo asado, y haras
torrijas de pan, y iras armando tu sopa
có torrijas y solomo, y salchichas y perdizes: han de ser hechas quartos las perdizes, y el solomo hecho pedaços: e iras
poniendo todo este recaudo en lechos,
y como fueres echando las torrijas y la
carne, iras echando queso rallado, y en
el queso echaras pimienta, y nuez, y xe-
gibre, y iras poniendo lechos hasta que
la sopa esté bien alta. Luego estrellaras
vnos hueuos que no sean muy duros, y
assentarlos has por encima la sopa: luego mojaras vn poco de queso có vn grano de ajo, y desatalo con caldo: luego
batiras en vn cazillo ocho hueuos, quatro con claras, y los otros quatro sin e-
llas, y batirlos has mucho, y desatalos
con caldo; luego echaras el caldo, y el
queso majado que esta en el almirez có
los hueuos, y echaras el caldo que te ¡a
recibir que sera menester para mojar
la sopa, y ponla sobre la lumbre, y trae
la a vna mano porque no se corre, y quá
do este espeso, sacalo del fuego, y velo
echando por encima de la sopa poco a
poco, de manera q se embeua muy bien,
y echale queso por encima. Ha de venira quedar la carne, y lo demas cubierto con la salsa, y ha de lleuar açafran, q
quede vn poco amarillo: y quando la
sopa estuuiere medio cozida, echale má-
teca de puerco por encima bien calien-

te, y queso rallado, y luego acabalo de
cozer en vn horno. Enellas capirotadas
se meten tambien aues, y anades, como
sean tiernas, porque es como olla podrida, que han de hallar muchas cosas en
ellas, y han de ser todas asadas primero.

echando queso rallado, y en el queso echaras pimiento, y nuez, y gengibre, y iras poniendo lechos hasta que la sopa este bien alta. Luego estrellaras unos huevos que no sean muy duros, y assentarlos has por encima la sops : luego mojaras un poco de queso con un grano de ajo, y desaralo con caldo : luego batiras en un cazillo ocho huevos, quatro con claras y los otros quatros sin ellas, batirlos has mucho, desaralos con caldo : luego echaras caldo, y el queso majado que está en el almirez con los huevos, , y echaras el caldo que te pareciere que sera menester para mojar la sopa, y ponla sobre la lumber, y trae la a una mano porque no se corre : y quando estè espeso, sacalo del fuego, y velo enchando por encima de las sopa poco a poco, de manera que se embeua muy bien, y echale queso por encima. Ha de venira quedar la carne, y lo demas cubierto con la salsa, y ha de llevar açafran, que quede un poco amarillo : y quando la sopa estuviere medio cozida, echale manteca de puerco encima bien caliente, y queso rallado, y luego acabalo de cozer en un horno. En estas capirotadasse meten Tambien aves, y anades, como sean tiernas, porque es como olla podrida, que han de hallar muchas cosas en ellas, y han de ser todas asadas primero.

Translation of Original Recipe

Take pork loin and sausages and partridges, all roasted, and you then make toasted bread strips, and you make your soup with the pork sirloin, and sausages and partridges which must be cut into quarters and the loin cut into small pieces, you lay the meats in layers in a pan with the toasted bread, sprinkle grated cheese on top, and on top of the cheese add pepper, nutmeg, and ginger, and layer until the dish is filled almost to the top. Then strew some not-very-hard-cooked eggs over the top of the dish: then crush a bit of cheese with some garlic, and mix it with some broth: then beat eight eggs in a bowl, four with the yolks and four without the whites, beat hard, and mix with broth: then mix the broth with eggs and the mixture with the cheese and garlic from the mortar and place over the fire, and bring it to a simmer: when it is thick, remove the pot from the fire, and pour over the top of the dish with the meat, covering it well, sprinkle cheese over the top. Leave the meat and cover the rest with the sauce, add saffron so it stays a little bit yellow: when the dish is half cooked, spread hot pork fat over the top and more cheese and finish cooking the dish in the oven. In this *capirotada*, cooks also put chickens and ducks, because they're tender, this is like *Olla Podrida*, in which you find many different things, but you must roast everything first.

Step 3. **Ingredients in original recipe:**

 Pork loin

🐢 Sausages

🐢 Partridges

🐢 Eggs

🐢 Bread

🐢 Ginger

🐢 Garlic

🐢 Broth

🐢 Cheese

🐢 Saffron

🐢 Lard

Step 4. Equipment, procedures required, action words:

🖐 Baking dish large enough to layer ingredients

🖐 Pots for broth and sauce

🖐 Grater

🖐 Knife

🖐 Oven

🖐 Chopping

🖐 Grating

🖐 Boiling

🖐 Roasting

Step 5. Unclear words and language:

The chronology of the recipe doesn't make sense by modern standards.

Sauce thickness is a guess: how liquid should it be?

The partridges/chickens would be small, but given the preparation of the other meats, it seems logical to shred the meat off the chicken.

Cooking time is unclear. Since all the ingredients are cooked, oven time probably refers to just enough time to heat everything through and melt the cheese.

What about the cheese? What type of cheese would most likely have been used? Perhaps a sheep's milk cheese that melts easily.

Again, you'll find many scribal abbreviations in the original recipe.

Step 6. **Resources used to clarify wordage, procedure, other issues:**

In modern Mexican cuisine, *capirotada* garners up visions of a sweet, wine-infused bread pudding bursting with raisins.

In Martínez Montiño's day, *capirotada* was another dish altogether, as this recipe illustrates. He indicates that the dish resembles an *Olla Podrida*, which was a layered soup-like dish.

Eggs, according to Carolyn A. Nadeau, played a vital role in Spanish cuisine at the time. (See "Spain, Culinary and General History" in **Selected Bibliographical Resources** for works by Nadeau.)

For comparison, pages 96-97 of Karen Hess's edition of *The Virginia House-wife* detail a similar concoction, "To Make an Olla—A Spanish Dish." Mary Randolph requires the addition of "apples or pears peeled and cut in two, tomatas [sic]," etc. She calls for a small amount of water, indicating that this 1824 version was not a stew. Robert May also included a recipe for Spanish *Olla Podrida*.

Recall Sancho Panza's *Olla Podrida* moment in Cervantes's *Don Quijote*, recounted by Penelope Casas on page 139 of her classic, *The Foods and Wines of Spain*.

The name "Capriotada" comes from the name of a priest's hat.

Step 7. **Notes regarding the final dish, what you would redo, change:**

Chicken substitutes well for the partridges, although you might want to consider using quails or Cornish hens instead.

Step 8. **Modern version of the recipe:**

    2   pounds pork shoulder

1   pound Spanish sausages

1   whole chicken, about 3½ pounds, quartered

    Olive oil for frying

1   loaf dense white country bread, in ½-inch slices

3   cups cheese, grated

4   eggs, hard-cooked and chopped

4   cups meat broth

½   teaspoon saffron, crushed

4   garlic cloves, peeled and finely minced in a mortar

4   whole eggs

4   egg whites

1   teaspoon ground black pepper, or to taste

¼   teaspoon ground nutmeg, or to taste

½   teaspoon ground ginger, or to taste

¼   cup lard, melted

Preheat oven to 425°F.

Place meats on a lightly greased baking sheet with 2-to-3-inch-high edges. As each meat is done, remove it from the baking sheet and place on a platter. While the meat roasts, fry the bread slices in the olive oil until golden brown. Place bread on another platter. Make the broth by adding the garlic and saffron. Bring the broth to a boil, reduce heat, and simmer for about 20 minutes. Beat whole eggs and whites together. Take a large, deep baking dish, rub with lard. Cut the pork into ½-inch slices. Shred the chicken into bite-size slices. Cut the sausage into chunks about 1½ inches thick. Begin layering the meat in the baking dish, followed by a layer of bread, sprinkle with cheese and spices. Repeat until you've layered it all. Stir the beaten eggs into the broth until the liquid thickens. Pour the broth mixture over the layered ingredients. Sprinkle with more of the cheese. Bake until half cooked through, remove from oven, and pour melted lard over the top. Continue baking until golden brown. Top with the chopped hard-cooked eggs. Cut into serving pieces and plate. Serves 6 or more.

NUEVO ARTE

F 13074 DE

COCINA,

SACADO

DE LA ESCUELA

DE LA

EXPERIENCIA

ECONOMICA,

SU AUTHOR

JUAN ALTAMIRAS.

Con las Licencias neceſſarias.

Barcelona: En la Imprenta de Maria Angela
Martì Viuda, en la Plaza de S. Jayme.
Año 1767.

Juan Altamiras,
Nuevo arte de la cocina Española

My life began in 1709, in La Almunia, a village in Aragon. The priest christened me with the name of Raimundo Gómez. By the time I was born, the eighth of ten children, my mother Catalina could count on much help in the kitchen. Her father, my grandfather, worked as a confectioner, making many types of glorious sweets that I loved to swipe off his work bench when he attended to the many pots bubbling on the hearth. I much preferred stirring the hot sugar to beating at olive trees during harvest time on my father's land! My heart, and God, commanded me to make my vows as a lay friar with the Franciscans. So I did. My Lord called me to the kitchens of San Lorenzo and San Cristóbal at first. The bounty of the table, the breaking of bread in community, all that transports the soul toward heaven. Eating makes a dark day come alive, at least for a moment.

Mestre Robert's book, *Libre del Coch,* also breathed joy into my life, and my kitchen. I also found inspiration and much to savor in Martínez Montiño's *Arte de Cocina,* seeing that he cooked in the palace of the Hapsburgs!

After many years, I cooked at the Colegio de San Diego de Zaragoza, its splendid garden of vegetables and fruit trees inspiring me. The young monks who attended the Colegio, homesick and in need of nourishment, sometimes yearned for more than just the solace of prayer. It was for them that I wrote my book *Nuevo arte de cocina, sacado de la Escuela de Experiencia Ecónomica* (The New Art of Cookery, Derived from the School of Economic Experience). My little book is not one for the king's or noble's table. Indeed not. It is the poor man I envisioned as I sat quietly in the darkness of night and penned the words for these dishes, with "charity's golden voice."

Step 1: **Recipe name and source:** *Pollos de Carretero, con Salsa de Pobres, Nuevo arte de la cocina Española* **(1745)**

Step 2: **Original recipe and translation:**

Este es un modo de componer Pollos promptos, y gustosos. Despues de bien limpios, haras quartos, los freiràs con tocino, ù con aceyta; tendràs un puchero de agua sazonada de sal, machacaràs ajos de modo que sobresalgan con pimienta, agràs, y azafrin; todo esto los machacaras junto, desatalo con el agua del puchero, que de dos hervores, con un puñado de pan rallado; tendrás los Pollos compuestos en una tortera, los echaràs la salsa por encima, que dèn otros dos hervores, teniendo cuydado de menearlos, no se socorren. Estos son unos Pollos, que se corre priessa, se pueden componer en media hora, por que de la sartèn salen el modo, que se pueden comer: la salsa sirve para suavizarlos, y abultarlos.

Translation of Original Recipe

Chicken in the Style of Carreteros, with Peppery "Poor Man's" Sauce

Note: "Carretero" refers to "cartwright" or "wagoneer," and the English name—"Carter"—grew out of the occupation of carting goods or people form one place to another. Altamiras's recipe likely had nothing to do with carters per se. It may just be that he associated them with something about the recipe.

This is a method for cooking chicken that's delicious and full of flavor. After rinsing the chicken, cut it into quarters and fry with bacon and some oil. Take a pan with salted water, crush together garlic with black pepper, verjuice, and saffron; add this to the boiling water with some grated bread. Lay the chicken in a shallow baking dish and pour the sauce over the top. Shake the pan to keep the chicken from burning. For those with little time, this dish only takes half an hour to cook with this method and is ready to eat. The sauce adds punch to the dish and serves to make the chicken more tender.

Step 3. **Ingredients in original recipe:**

     Chicken

     Bacon

- 🧅 Oil
- 🧅 Salt
- 🧅 Garlic
- 🧅 Black pepper
- 🧅 Verjuice
- 🧅 Saffron

STEP 4. Equipment, procedures required, action words:

- 🧅 Knife
- 🧅 Pan for frying
- 🧅 Baking dish
- 🧅 Mortar/crusher
- 🧅 Grater
- 🧅 Frying
- 🧅 Cutting
- 🧅 Baking

Step 5. Unclear words and language:

🌿 The black pepper is the key to this dish and the amount is unclear. A highly peppered dish in Tuscany—*Peposo*—may be a cousin to this dish.

🌿 Using a modern recipe as a guideline, with two tablespoons of crushed peppercorns, seemed a bit excessive. Start with a smaller amount and working your way up according to taste works best.

🌿 Use vinegar if you cannot locate a source of verjuice.

🌿 What type of cookware—ceramic or metal?

Step 6. Resources used to clarify wordage, procedure, other issues:

🌿 Tuscan cookbooks

🍀 Alicia Rios's *Heritage of Spanish Cooking*

🍀 Vicky Hayward's interpretation. See *Art of Cookery: A Spanish Friar's Kitchen Notebook.*

🍀 Cookware—check Diego Velázquez's 1618 painting, "Old Woman Frying Eggs," dish appears to be ceramic.

🍀 Altamiras cooked during the period of the Spanish Enlightenment. Much French influence in Spain at the time, due to the presence of Bourbon rulers.

Step 7. Notes regarding the final dish, what you would redo, change:

More pepper is better!

Step 8. Modern version of the recipe:

3	slices center-cut bacon
2	tablespoons olive oil
1	3½-pound frying chicken, cut into quarter after removing backbone
4	cloves garlic, peeled and finely chopped
½	tablespoon sherry vinegar
2	cups broth, salted
½	teaspoon saffron
½	tablespoon ground black peppercorns
¾	cup dry bread crumbs, preferably homemade or from a solid loaf, not wispy bakery bread
¼	cup chopped parsley
1	tablespoon lard, for greasing baking dish with a cover

Preheat oven to 375°F.

In a skillet, fry the bacon in the oil until crisp. Set bacon aside on a plate. Brown the chicken in the fat in the pan. Place chicken in single layer in the greased baking dish. Add bread crumbs to the skillet and stir for 1 minute. Add the minced garlic and chopped parsley. Stir in stock, vinegar, and saffron. Pour the sauce over the chicken, cover, and bake about an hour. As the original recipe states, this is a dish that can be prepared quickly when time is short. It can be cooked on top of the stove, too, with the cook making sure that the heat is kept low enough to prevent burning. To serve, dish up chicken quarters onto individual plates and spoon sauce over the top. Serves 4.

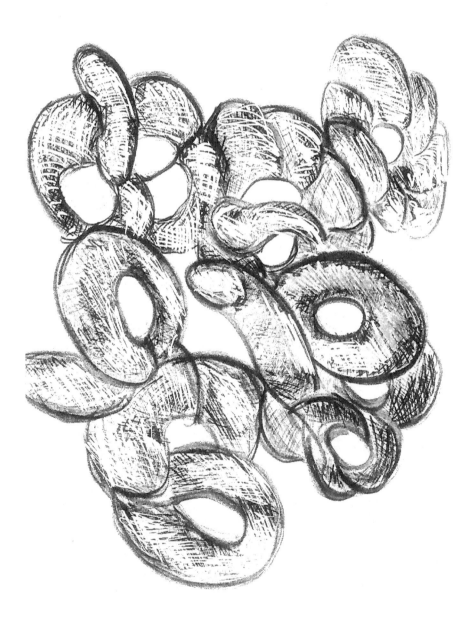

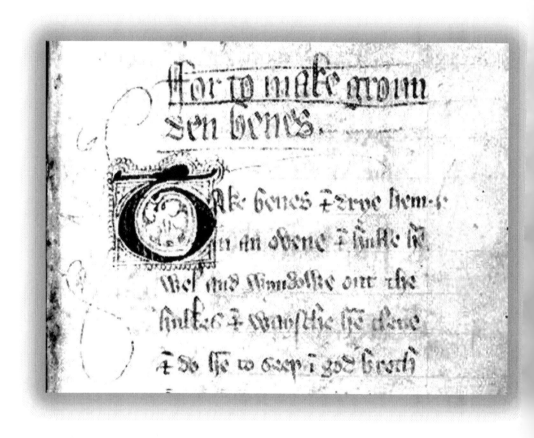

Portion of The Forme of Cury, for Benes Yfryed (Fried Beans)

Chapter 13

Step-by-Step Analysis: English Cookbooks

The Forme of Cury

My lord, King Richard II, took me to his service as Master Cook. He is a grand *seigneur*, perhaps the best of all the Christian kings. His table always boasts the latest delicacies, even when he journeys from one estate to another, far and wide across this green land of England. He especially loves the magnificent sotelties that my cooks and I cre-

ate for him, solid castles raised high with coffin dough. In the year 1390, my lord beseeched me to lay down on vellum with my pen the many dishes that warm his heart on cold evenings of cease-less rain.

So I did, with the help of my men. To benefit the young lads new to the travail of the kitchen, I wrote the receipts with plentiful attention to the ingredients, the method of cooking, and added a word or two about the way the King prefers his food to be served at table.

When word seeped out that we'd recorded our kitchen's secrets, all and sundry came, slyly begging for a glimpse of the 196 recipes we scratched on the vellum, made from the finest of calf skin.

Oh, the luxury of serving the lords and their ladies such dishes as porpoises, cranes, herons, and seals! Gold leaf, the finest of the fine, we use all that to flourish the messes of the King. The health of the King we forebear, with advice from the learned doctors of physick. Safroun finds its way into our pots, and yellows what it touches at will.

Step 1. **Recipe name and source: Capouns In Councys, from *The Forme of Cury* (1390)**

Step 2. **Original recipe and transcription:**

Capouns In Councys. XXII. *Take Capons and rost hem right hoot þat þey be not half y nouhz and hewe hem to gobettes and cast hem in a pot, do þerto clene* broth, *seeþ hem þat þey be tendre. Take brede and þe self broth and drawe it up yferer, take strong Powdour and* **Safroun** and Salt and cast þer to. *Take ayrenn and seeþ hem harde. Take out the zolkes and hewe the whyte* þerinne, *take the Pot fro þe fyre and cast the whyte þerinne. Messe the dishes* þerwith *and lay the ʒolkes hool and flour it with clowes.*

Transliteration of Recipe

Take capons and roast them right hot that they not be half enough or half done and chop them into pieces and cast them into a pot in thereto clean broth, boil them till they be tender. Take bread and the same broth and place it all on the fire, take strong powder and saffron and salt and cast thereto. Take eggs and seethe them hard. Take out the yolks and chop the whites therein, take the pot from the fire and cast the whites therein. Lay out the dishes therewith and lay the whole yolks and flour/sprinkle the dish with cloves.

Step 3. **Ingredients in original recipe:**

- Cloves: an extremely expensive ingredient during the Middle Ages.

- Eggs
- Chickens
- "Strong Powder" (*Poudre Forte*)
- Saffron
- Bread
- Broth
- Lard

Step 4. **Equipment, procedures required, action words:**

- Pot for broth
- Roasting pan

- Knife
- Chopping

- Boiling
- Roasting

Step 5. **Unclear words and language:**

- The use of the "thorn" letter may cause some difficulty here: "þat þey" means "that they," for example.

- Another letter is "yough," as in 3olkes, where the letter is often transliterated as a "z." It more closely resembles a "3."

- "Half enough" means "half done."

- "Strong powder" (*Poudre Forte*)

- Sotelties

- Coffin

- Messes

Step 6. **Resources used to clarify wordage, procedure, other issues:**

🍒 Old English and Anglo-Saxon dictionaries

🍒 *Poudre Forte*:

1½	tablespoons ground ginger
1	tablespoon ground cinnamon
½	teaspoon ground mace
½	teaspoon ground cloves
½	teaspoon fresh ground black pepper
½	teaspoon grains of paradise, ground with a mortar and pestle (optional)

Mix everything together and store in air-tight container in dark, dry place.

● Sotelties: a dish made to look like something else. Fish made to look like meat, etc.

● Coffin: a thick pastry meant to encase a filling

● Messes: originating as a French word for courses during a meal, *mes* appeared in Middle English (1250-1330 A.D.)

● Other versions of the recipe:

Capon in couns (from *A Noble Boke Off Cookry*)

Capouns in councy (from *Fourme of Curye* [Rylands MS 7])

Capons in Covisye (from *Liber cure cocorum* [Sloane MS 1986])

Caponys in concys (from MS Douce 257)

Step 7. **Notes regarding the final dish, what you would redo, change:**

To please modern tastes, sprinkle a bit of freshly chopped parsley over the top just before serving, along with the ground cloves.

Step 8. **Modern version of the recipe:**

4	eggs, hard-cooked
1	5-pound chicken
1	tablespoon lard

3   cups chicken broth, low-salt or salt-free

2   garlic cloves, peeled and minced

2   tablespoons chopped fresh parsley

½   cup dry bread crumbs, preferably homemade from a solid loaf, not wispy bakery bread

½   teaspoon strong powder (*Poudre Forte*)

Pinch saffron

Salt and ground black pepper to taste

Ground cloves to taste

Preheat your oven to 375°F.

Dry chicken with a clean paper towel, rub the skin with some of the lard, and sprinkle with salt and pepper. Place chicken in a baking dish greased with the rest of the lard. Roast chicken for 1 hour at 375°F, then reduce heat to 350°F and cook for another hour. Meanwhile, prepare the stock. Pour broth into a large pot, add garlic and parsley. Simmer for 30 minutes. Set aside. When chicken is done, cut it into serving pieces. Remove the yolks from the eggs and chop the whites. Stir the bread crumbs into the stock and add the saffron. Add the chicken pieces, strong powder, and chopped egg whites. Simmer for 15–20 minutes. Stock will thicken, and you may need to add more broth to make the dish the consistency of a thick soup. Add salt and pepper to taste. Put chicken and stock into a large serving dish. Crumble the egg yolks and strew over the top of the chicken. To finish, sprinkle a small amount of ground cloves over the chicken. Serves 6.

167

¶ A Proper

newe Booke of Cokerye,
Declarynge what maner of
meates be beste in seafon,
for al times in the yere,
and how they ought
to be dreſſed, and
ſerued at the ta
ble, bothe for
fleſhe dayes,
and fyſhe
dayes.
With a newe addition, verye ne=
ceſſarye for all them that
delyghteth in Co=
kerye .

(❧)

A Proper Newe Booke of Cokerye

Margaret Parker is my name. Or Meg, if you please. You need not fuss your head with the details of my association with this book, for I am but a humble wife, blessed with the gift of reading. Thus I share with my cooks all the riches to be found in *A Proper Newe Booke of Cokerye, declarynge what maner of Meates beste be in season, for al times in the yere, and How They Ought To be dressed, and serued at the table for bothe fleshe dayes, and Fyshe dayes. With a new addition, which is necessary for all those whom delyghteth in Cokerye*, which enlightens the minds of many ladies, including my own.

I call upon this book when serving dinners to the many men who come to my household as guests of my husband, Matthew Parker, the fourteenth Master of Corpus Christi College in Cambridge, and later the Archbishop of Canterbury. The lavishness of some of those evenings nearly brought my cook to her knees! Here consider a bill of fare:

The first course

Potage or stewed broth

Boylde meate or stewed meate

Chyckens and baken

Powdered beife

Pies

Goose

Pigge

Rosted Beefe

Rosted Veale

Custarde

The second course

Rosted Lambe

Rosted Capons

Rosted Connies

Chickens

Pehennes

Baken Venyson. Tarte

Of course, on fish days, no such opulence reigns! And I recall with fondness the damsons, strawberries, medlars, gooseberries, and wardens, pears of such golden hue I marvel at the hand of God for providing us with great bounty. All of these things the kind author of this little book of 50 recipes bequeathed to us. My husband especially loves the pie of greene apples.

Step 1. **Recipe name and source: To Make Pyes of Grene Apples, from** *A Proper Newe Booke of Cookery Newe Boke of Cokerye* **(1545)**

Step 2. **Original recipe and transcription:**

Take your Apples and pare them cleane, and core them as ye wil a quince then make your coffin after this manner, take a little fayre water, and halfe a fishe of butter, and a little Saffron, and set all this upon a chafindyshe, tyll it bee hote, than temper your flower with this sayd licour, and the white of two egges, & also make your coffin and season your Apples with Cinamon, Ginger and Sugar inough. Then put them into your coffin, and bake them.

Transcription of Recipe

Take your apples and peel them, and core them as you would a quince then make your pastry in this manner, take a little fair water, and half a dish of butter, and a little saffron, and set all this in a chafing dish, till it be hot, then temper your flour with this liquid, and the white of two eggs, and also make the pastry and season your apples with cinnamon, ginger and sugar enough (to taste). Then put them into your pastry, and bake them.

Step 3. **Ingredients in original recipe:**

- Apples: green
- Sugar
- Cinnamon
- Ginger
- Saffron
- Butter
- Flour

Step 4. **Equipment, procedures required, action words:**

- Implied: making a hot-water pastry. Rolling pin
- Peeling and slicing (apples).
- Deep dish needed for all the apples.

Step 5. **Unclear words and language:**

- Cinnamon, ginger, saffron: ground form (?), but obvious
- Apples should be whole or sliced? Should they really be green or just unripe? See Step 6.
- Baking time not given nor heat of the oven/fire

Step 6. **Resources used to clarify wordage, procedure, other issues:**

- *The good Huswifes Handmaide for the Kitchin* (1594) appears to require that the pippins (apples) be set whole inside the crust. Modern apples are bigger, so slicing works better here.

🍎 Check recipes online or in modern cookbooks such as *Joy of Cooking* for time and temperatures for deep-dish apple pies.

Step 7. Notes regarding the final dish, what you would redo, change:

🍎 Green apples such as Granny Smiths work well.

🍎 Use enough apples to completely fill the baking dish. Pastry needs to be filled completely and egg wash used to make top more glazed looking.

Step 8. Modern version of the recipe:

CRUST:

1   cup water

1/3   cup unsalted butter

     Pinch of saffron

3   cups all-purpose flour

½   cup whole wheat pastry flour

2   tablespoons granulated sugar

     Pinch of fine sea salt

1   egg, beaten

Preheat oven to 375°F.

Heat the water, butter, and saffron to boiling in a small pan. Mix flours, sugar, salt, and egg in a large mixing bowl. Pour in the hot water and stir vigorously with a wooden spoon. Remove the pastry to a floured surface and knead dough until smooth. Roll out three-fourths of the dough to fit a 9-inch springform, or other, pan. Place dough in pan, with some overhang. Reserve the rest of the dough for the top crust. Roll into a circle about one inch wider than your pan.

FILLING:

4   Granny Smith apples, peeled, cored and sliced

½   cup granulated sugar

½   teaspoon ground ginger

1   teaspoon ground cinnamon

2   egg whites, beaten

Mix all ingredients together in a large bowl. Scrape mixture into prepared crust and moisten edges of dough with water. Place the top crust over the apples. Pinch the two crusts together and crimp. Brush top with the two egg yolks beaten with 1 tablespoon of water. Cut slits in top of dough. Bake for about half an hour at 375°F, then reduce heat to 350°F for another half hour. Cool in pan for 20 minutes, then remove rim of springform pan, if using. Before serving, cool completely.

N. 1400

THE ENGLISH Hus-wife,

Contayning,

The inward and outward vertues which
ought to be in a compleat woman.

As, her skill in Physicke, Cookery, Banqueting-
stuffe, Distillation, Perfumes, VVooll, Hemp, Flax,
Dayries, Brewing, Baking, *and all other things*
belonging to an Houshould.

A Worke very profitable and necessarie, gathered for
the generall good of this kingdome.

Printed at London by *Iohn Beale*, for *Roger Iackson*,
and are to bee sold at his shop neere the great
Cunduit in Fleet-streete. 1615.

Gervase Markham
The English Hus-wife

Note: By Gervase Markham's day, you could read the recipes and text more or less as modern-day English, without resorting to a dictionary or glossary.

My mother told me of my birth, which came to pass sometime in the year 1568. As I was the third son of my father, I had no prospects. Indeed, neither did he, for although he came from a noble family of Nottinghamshire, his fortunes deflated year by year. I took myself to Ireland and the Netherlands, a soldier for the Queen, Elizabeth I. Marriage to Mary Gellsthorpe in 1601 turned me into a *pater familias* with a horde of children. My grand household led me into many endeavors, including the breeding of those great Arabian horses.

With my pen, my light shone especially bright. Of all my books, perhaps *The English Hus-wife*, part of *Country Contentments*, satisfied me and my readers the most. I wrote about horses, cattle, and cookery, among many other topics. My cookery followed the English manner, from first to last. "[An] honorable Personage of this kingdom" aided me greatly by sharing her receipt book. Let my words say it all, "… *let it be rather to satisfie nature then our affections, and apter to kill hunger then revive new appetites, let it proceed more from the provision of her owne yarde, than the furniture of the markets; and let it be rather esteemed for the familiar acquaintance she hath with it, then for the strangenesse and raritie it bringeth from other Countries.*"[44]

One day I made my way to the London docks, watching the dockers loading a ship bound for the New World. One docker caught my eye. Sweat rolled down his cheeks and blinded him for a minute as he grabbed for the dirty white cloth around his neck. He wiped his face with the foul, sweaty rag. A last wooden chest lay at his feet, destined for the ship *Supply*. A friend told me that George Thorpe expected a copy of my book, *The English Hus-wife*, when that ship docked at Jamestown, in far-away Virginia. Perhaps more copies in lay in that trunk that same day!

That book, and my love of horses—for I was the first to import an Arabian horse into England—both these things I view as my greatest legacy. Wagging tongues say that Will Shakespeare lampooned me, as Don Adriano de Armado in "Love's Labour Lost." So be it. Fie on him!

Step 1. **Recipe name and source: A Prune Tart, from** *The English Hus-wife* **(1615)**

Step 2. **Original recipe and transcription:**

Take of the fairest damask prunes you can get, and put them in a clean pipkin[45] with fair water, sugar, unbruised cinnamon, and a branch or two of rosemary; and if you have bread to bake, stew them in the oven with your bread, if otherwise, stew them on the fire; when they are stewed them all to mash in their syrup, and strain them into a clean dish; then boil it over again with sugar, cinnamon, and rose-water till it be as thick as marmalade; then set to cool, then make a tough paste with fine flour, water, and a little butter, and roll it out very thin, then, having patterns of paper cut in divers proportions, as beasts, birds, arms, knots, flowers, and such like, lay the patterns on the paste, and so cut them accordingly; then with your fingers pinch up the edges of the paste, and set the work in good proportion: then prick it well all over for rising, and set on a clean sheet of large paper, and so set it into the oven, and bake it hard: then draw, and set it by to cool: and thus you may do by a whole oven full at one time, as your occasion of expense is: then against the time of service comes, take off the confection of prunes before rehearsed, and with your knife, or a spoon, fill the coffin according to the thickness of the verge: then strew it over all with caraway comfits, and prick long comfits upright in it, and so, taking the paper from the bottom, serve it on a plate in a dish or charger, according to bigness of the tart, and at the second course, and this tart carrieth the colour black.

Step 3. Ingredients in original recipe:

- Prunes
- Sugar
- Cinnamon
- Rosemary
- Caraway comfits
- Rosewater
- Pastry

Step 4. Equipment, procedures required, action words:

- Rolling dough and cutting it
- Boiling
- Mashing
- Straining
- Reducing
- Rolling pin
- Pot for boiling
- Shallow pan for reducing
- Tart tin

Step 5. Unclear words and language:

- Fair water?
- Fineness of sieve for prunes. A *chinois* makes it quite difficult to get much pulp into the final mixture. (See endnote 45 for more about a *chinois*.)
- Damask prunes, made from plums? Could the tart be made from fresh fruit?

🐓 Caraway comfits: seeds and log-like version?

🐓 How did cooks cut the paper shapes/patterns?

Step 6. Resources used to clarify wordage, procedure, other issues:

🐓 Fair water = clean water

🐓 The ending of the last sentence—"carrieth the color black"—does this signify one of the four humor categories in any way? "Melancholy?"

🐓 Black color: ensures that the author means dried prunes, not fresh.

🐓 Refer to Gilly Lehmann's *The British Housewife* for more about comfits. The word "comfits" refers to nuts, seeds, and fruits coated with sugar. "Confits" refers to food items preserved in a liquid or other substance, such as duck confit, where melted fat serves as the immersion substance.

Step 7. Notes regarding the final dish, what you would redo, change:

🐓 Use cookie cutters for pastry shapes, as these lend more consistency than do paper patterns.

🐓 The seed version of the caraway comfits infuses too much of a caraway taste. You might prefer placing a bowl of the comfits on the table and let each person sprinkle their own on top of their individual serving. Use a minimal amount of sugar syrup while coating the seeds.

Step 8. Modern version of the recipe:

FILLING

6 cups dried, pitted prunes

2½ cups water

1 3-inch cinnamon stick

1 4-inch-long sprig of fresh rosemary

½ cup granulated sugar

1   tablespoon rosewater

¼   cup granulated sugar

¾   teaspoon ground cinnamon

In a medium saucepan, heat the prunes in the 2½ cups of water with the cinnamon stick, rosemary, and sugar until boiling. Lower heat and simmer for 30 minutes, or until prunes soften and you can easily mash them. Stir occasionally to prevent sticking. If sticking, add small amounts of water. Mash prunes in their syrup and strain into a clean bowl through a *chinois* or other fine mesh strainer. Note that this requires patience and some muscle power! Discard the skins and pulp. Reserve the smooth purée.

When you've strained the prunes, scrape the purée into a clean skillet. Heat the mixture to low boil, add the rosewater, ¼ cup granulated sugar, and ground cinnamon. Stirring constantly, cook the purée down until it's the consistency of a thick marmalade. Remove from heat and set aside. Let cool. Scrape into cooled tart shell. Top with the baked cutouts. Sprinkle with caraway comfits, if desired. Serve these comfits in a small dish, allowing people to add as many, or as few, as they desire with their individual serving.

TART CRUST (Makes two 9-inch crusts)

1¼   cups all-purpose flour

1¼   cups whole wheat pastry flour

¼   teaspoon fine sea salt

2/3   cup unsalted butter, cut into small cubes

3–4 tablespoons cold water

Preheat oven to 375°F.

Stir flours together with the salt. Add the butter and mix in with your fingers or a pastry cutter until the mixture resembles rough bread crumbs. Sprinkle in water, one tablespoon at a time. Stir well. Add water until dough comes together well when you make a ball shape with the dough. Cut ball into two sections. Flatten into ½-inch-thick disks on wax paper or parchment paper. Wrap in the paper and cool in the refrigerator for about 10 minutes. Roll out disks to approximately 10–11 inches in diameter between sheets of wax paper. Cool in refrigerator for another 10 minutes. Remove wax paper and place one disk into 9-inch tart tin. Smooth off edges by running a rolling pin over the excess dough protruding from the tin. Prick crust with a fork and line the dough aluminum foil. Weigh it down with some dried beans or pie weights. Place tart crust in your oven and let cook for about 15 minutes with the foil and beans. Remove the foil and beans after that time and bake for another 20 minutes, more or less, until crust is lightly brown on the top of the edges. Remove from oven and cool

With the second disk of dough, roll out 10-to-11 inches in diameter. Cut out decorative shapes with a sharp knife, using patterns or a freehand design. Use cookie cutters if desired. Place cutout on baking sheet covered with parchment paper and bake in the oven for close to 20 minutes or until lightly golden in color. When cool, place on top of the tart filling and serve.

CARAWAY COMFITS

½   cup granulated sugar

3   tablespoons water

2   tablespoons caraway seeds

Make syrup with sugar and water. Heat to boiling, let boil about 1 minute, or until syrup temperature reads 225°F on an instant-read thermometer. Put seeds into a small, non-stick skillet and heat over medium-low heat. When you can feel the heat, but it doesn't hurt, add a scant ½ teaspoon of the syrup to the seeds and stir until you don't see any gleaming from the sugar syrup. Let seeds dry in the low heat before adding more syrup. Repeat this procedure 11 times. You will see the sugar crusting on the seeds. When you're done, put the seeds on a clean plate and let sit in a cool dry place for about two hours. Then store in a glass jar in a cool dry place for a week or so.

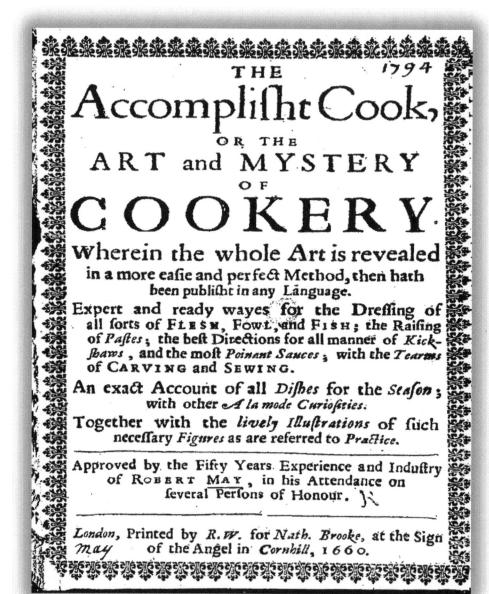

THE

1794

Accomplisht Cook,

OR THE

ART and MYSTERY

OF

COOKERY.

Wherein the whole Art is revealed
in a more easie and perfect Method, then hath
been publisht in any Language.

Expert and ready wayes for the Dressing of
all sorts of FLESH, FOWL, and FISH; the Raising
of *Pastes*; the best Directions for all manner of *Kick-
shaws*, and the most *Poinant Sauces*; with the *Tearms*
of CARVING and SEWING.

An exact Account of all *Dishes* for the *Season*;
with other *A la mode Curiosities.*

Together with the *lively Illustrations* of such
necessary *Figures* as are referred to *Practice.*

Approved by the Fifty Years Experience and Industry
of ROBERT MAY, in his Attendance on
several Persons of Honour.

London, Printed by R. W. for *Nath. Brooke*, at the Sign
May   of the Angel in *Cornhill*, 1660.

Robert May
The Accomplisht Cook

My father always said I came into the world with a stirring spoon in my right hand. The Spanish Armada sank the same year, 1588, but that event didn't affect my father's position as cook to Lady Dormer. I myself worked for Lady Dormer and many other families of the Catholic gentry and nobility in my long career. Although my father taught me much, I made my way to Paris, the source of much refined cooking.

After the five years of toil I spent there, I returned to England, wondering what my future held. Then Arthur Hollinsworth of the Star Chamber[46] took me on as an apprentice in Newgate Market and introduced me to the Worshipful Company of Cooks.[47] The years passed, and the wonders of New World unfolded before me in the kitchen. I learned of the cooking of Spain and Italy. Combined with knowledge I gleaned of French dishes from my Paris years, my cooking skills took me to some of the most well-equipped and stocked kitchens in England. For a while, I cooked for Elizabeth Grey, Countess of Kent, who later wrote *A True Gentlewoman's Delight* (1653). Truth be told, the Civil War and the Protectorate cast a pall over of many of the pleasures of the past.

With the Restoration of the monarchy under Charles II beginning in 1660, I felt the time well suited to publish my cookery book, *The Accomplisht Cook*. My *olla podrida*, or "olio," commences the revelation of my secrets. Almost 1000 receipts, my "jewels," if you will. Potatoes from the New World. That grand bird, the turkey, as well. With just one Bill of Fare for Fish Days, I lay before the feet of my readers the glories of meat and sauces and other such dishes as Fritters of Spinage.

Even though I spent some years among the French, and admired their cooking, I remained English to my core. French chefs "by their insinuations, not without enough of ignorance, [they] have bewitcht some of the gallants of our nation with epigram dishes... their mushroom'd experiences for sauce rather than diet, for the generality howsoever called A-la mode, not so worthy of being taken notice of."[48]

Step 1. **Recipe name and source: Fritters of Spinage (Spinach Fritters), from** *The Accomplisht Cook* **(1660)**

Step 2: **Original recipe:**

Take spinage, pick it and wash it, then set on a skillet of fair water, and when it boileth put in the spinage, being tender boil'd put it in a cullender (colander) to drain away the liquor (liquid); then mince it small (fine) on a fair board, put it in a dish and season it with cinamon, ginger, grated manchet, fix eggs with the whites and yolks, a little cream or none, make the stuff pretty thick, and put in some boil'd currans. Fry it by spoonfuls, and serve it on a dish and plate with sugar.

Thus also you may make fritters of beets, clary, borage, bugloss, or lattice.

Step 3. **Ingredients in original recipe:**

- Spinach
- Cinnamon
- Ginger
- Bread crumbs
- Eggs
- Cream

Step 4. **Equipment, procedures required, action words:**

- Pot
- Colander
- Knife
- Grater
- Whipper
- Boiling
- Mincing
- Whipping (beating)

153

Step 5. Unclear words and language:

> How much spinach?

> Do you whip the egg whites separately from the yolks, given that this resulted in lighter batters until the common use of baking powder in the nineteenth century?

Step 6. Resources used to clarify wordage, procedure, other issues:

> Modern fritter recipes? A glance at a modern recipe revealed that May's recipe looks about the same, except that the modern recipe doesn't include sugar. Rather, grated cheese provides the seasoning.

> Sugar, during May's time, acted as a status symbol and an ingredient in medicinal treatments.

Step 7. Notes regarding the final dish, what you would redo, change:

> Add more eggs, if batter seems too thick. Whip egg whites separately and fold in for a lighter result.

> Use another green leafy vegetable if desired.

> These fritters resemble small zucchini breads.

Step 8. Modern version of the recipe:

2	bunches of fresh spinach, or about 1.5 pounds
½	teaspoon sea salt
1/3	cup golden raisins that have been boiled and drained
1½–2	cups finely pulverized stale white bread
3	tablespoons heavy cream
2	eggs, beaten
½	teaspoon ground cinnamon
¼	teaspoon ground ginger
1½	cups vegetable oil
	Confectioner's sugar

Wash and drain the spinach, removing most of the stems. Add the spinach to a pot of boiling water seasoned with the salt. Cook approximately 3 minutes at a boil. Drain well and when cool, wrap spinach in a clean towel and squeeze out the excess liquid. Chop spinach finely and place in large mixing bowl. Add remaining ingredients except for oil and sugar. Mixture should be thick, but still slightly fluid. Heat oil in high-sided skillet. Drop batter in by soup spoonfuls, about two tablespoons. Cook until golden brown and floating on top of oil. Turn once during cooking. When done, remove from oil with a slotted spoon. Drain on paper towel. When cooled slightly, sprinkle with a heavy coating of confectioner's sugar by using a small sieve. Best when cooled almost completely. Makes 18-24, depending on the size of your spoons.

A R T

OF

C O O K E R Y,

Made PLAIN and EASY;

Which far exceeds any THING of the Kind ever yet Publifhed.

CONTAINING,

I. Of Roafting, Boiling, &c.
II. Of Made-Difhes.
III. Read this Chapter, and you will find how Expenfive a French Cook's Sauce is.
IV. To make a Number of pretty little Difhes fit for a Supper, or Side-Difh, and little Corner-Difhes for a great Table; and the reft you have in the Chapter for Lent.
V. To drefs Fifh.
VI. Of Soops and Broths.
VII. Of Puddings.
VIII. Of Pies.
IX. For a Faft-Dinner, a Number of good Difhes, which you may make ufe for a Table at any other Time.
X. Directions for the Sick.
XI. For Captains of Ships.
XII. Of Hog's Puddings, Saufages, &c.

XIII. To Pot and Make Hams, &c.
XIV. Of Pickling.
XV. Of Making Cakes, &c.
XVI. Of Cheefecakes, Creams, Jellies, Whip Syllabubs, &c.
XVII. Of Made Wines, Brewing, French Bread, Muffins, &c.
XVIII. Jarring Cherries, and Preferves, &c.
XIX. To Make Anchovies, Vermicella, Ketchup, Vinegar, and to keep Artichokes, French-Beans, &c.
XX. Of Diftilling.
XXI. How to Market, and the Seafons of the Year for Butcher's Meat, Poultry, Fifh, Herbs, Roots, &c. and Fruit.
XXII. A certain Cure for the Bite of a Mad Dog. By Dr. Mead.

BY A LADY.

LONDON:

Printed for the AUTHOR; and fold at Mrs. *Afhburn's*, a China-Shop, the Corner of *Fleet-Ditch*. MDCCXLVII.

Hannah Glasse
The Art of Cookery, Made Plain and Easy

I am a bastard. Mother, the widow Mrs. Hannah Reynolds, fell into relationship lasting many years, or at least as long enough for my two siblings to see the light of day and join me on Earth. My half-brother, Lancelot, born in 1711 to my father's true wife, three years after myself, became my family. Lancelot served as M.P. for our district in his later years.[49] My mother was a dreadful harridan, bitter due to Life's fortunes disappointing her expectations. My father, Isaac Allgood of Hexham, Northumberland, a landowner, died in 1725, a year after I married John Glasse, a dashing soldier and irresistible to my 16-year-old-heart. My fleeting prosperity came from my father's passing.

And John spent it all.

My husband, may God rest his soul, failed to provide well for us. Though he could certainly make babies. Eleven times I sat on the birthing stool, yet just five of my wee ones survived past their fifth year.

So, despite my terrible spelling, I took up my pen and wrote *The Art of Cookery, Made Plain and Easy*, which I published in 1747. To my delight, it went into two editions. Readers clamored for it, no doubt finding the recipes of greater ease to prepare, a difference from such books *Whole Duty of a Woman*. I confess I found much meat for my own book in that tome.

When John died in 1749, I needed money. After all, I still had a three-year-old child at home. Selling Daffy's Elixir came to naught, as did the first shop. I sold my copyright to solve my bankruptcy problems. I opened another shop, of habits, where the rich and famous sought fancy clothing. My debts piled up again and my fortunes plummeted. I shamed myself and my family by being forced into debtors' prison in 1757. To add to my woes, in 1760, Ann Cook sullied my name in her book *The Professed Cook*, for she believed my brother Lancelot had done her family ill. But I take solace in knowing that my book reached cooks all the way across the Atlantic, that it sits on shelves and in hands in that far away New World.

Step 1. Recipe name and source: **To Dress a Loin of Pork with Onions from** *The Art of Cookery, Made Plain and Easy* **(1747)**

Step 2. Original recipe:

To dress a Loin of Pork with onions: Take a Fore-Loin of Pork and roast it, as at another time, peel a Quarter of a Peck of Onions, and slice them thin, lay them in the Dripping pan, which must be very clean, under the Pork, let the Fat drop on them; when the Pork is nigh enough, put the Onions into the sauce-pan, let them simmer over the Fire a Quarter of an Hour, shaking them well, then pour out all the Fat as well as you can, shake in a very little Flour, a Spoonful of Vinegar, and three Tea Spoonfuls of Mustard, shake all well together and stir in the Mustard, set it over the Fire for four or five Minutes, lay the Pork in a Dish and the Onions in a Bason. This is an admirable Dish to those who love Onions.

Step 3. Ingredients in original recipe:

- Pork loin
- Onions
- Flour
- Vinegar
- Mustard
- Drippings

Step 4. Equipment, procedures required, action words:

- Roasting pan
- Knife
- Spoon
- Bason (dish)
- Slicing
- Roasting
- Stirring

Step 5. Unclear words and language:

- Bason: early manner of spelling of basin

- Dripping pan: a shallow pan used to catch the drippings when a piece of meat roasts in a hearth

- Mustard: prepared? Make with water and ground mustard powder?

Step 6. Resources used to clarify wordage, procedure, other issues:

- Dictionary to check on "bason." *Oxford English Dictionary* not helpful. Glossary at the end of the Prospect Books edition of *The Art of Cookery, Made Plain and Easy*

- Mustard: prepared mustards available at the time.

- Robert May's recipe for a whole pig, page 146 of Prospect Books edition, seems to be based on a similar recipe in Markham.

Step 7. Notes regarding the final dish, what you would redo, change:

- Using a rolled and tied boneless pork shoulder roast results in a fattier, more succulent dish. You will be rewarded with more drippings as well for the sauce.

- The dish is not visually attractive, so strewing each plated serving with chopped parsley detracts from that!

Step 8. Modern version of the recipe:

Since modern pork is quite lean, you'll want to consider using a pork butt or shoulder roast instead of loin. See Step 7 above.

- 5½ pound pork butt roast, with fat left on
- 2½ pounds yellow onions, peeled and sliced ¼ inch think
- 1/3 cup lard
- 2–3 tablespoons flour
- 1 tablespoon cider vinegar
- 4 teaspoons Coleman's prepared mustard, plus 2 teaspoons grainy mustard

½–1 cup water

Salt and black pepper to taste

Chopped parsley (optional)

Roasting pan with rack

Preheat oven to 400°F.

Grease a roasting pan with a few teaspoons of the lard. Place a rack in the pan and set the roast on the rack, fat side up. Sprinkle the meat liberally with salt and black pepper. Roast for 15 minutes and reduce the heat to 350°F. Roast for 45 minutes more.

Meanwhile, peel and slice the onions. When the roast has been in oven for 45 minutes, remove it from the oven, take the roast out of the pan with the rack, add about 2 tablespoons of lard to the pan and let melt. Toss in the sliced onions and stir to cover them with the lard. Sprinkle with salt. Replace rack with the roast, return it to the oven, and continue baking for approximately 25 minutes per pound. You will need to stir the onions approximately every 30 minutes to ensure that the slices closest to the edges do not burn.

When an instant-read thermometer reads 145°F, remove pork from oven and let it sit while you make the onion sauce. Place the onions and drippings in a skillet and brown them a bit, for about 3 minutes over medium-high heat. Stir in the flour and allow to brown for a few minutes more. Add the vinegar, mustard, and water. Let the mixture bubble a few more minutes, then season with black pepper.

To serve, slice the pork and lay it on platter. Spoon the onions around the edges of the platter and garnish with chopped parsley. If you prefer, serve slices on plates, with onions spread over the top of the slices. Garnish with chopped parsley.

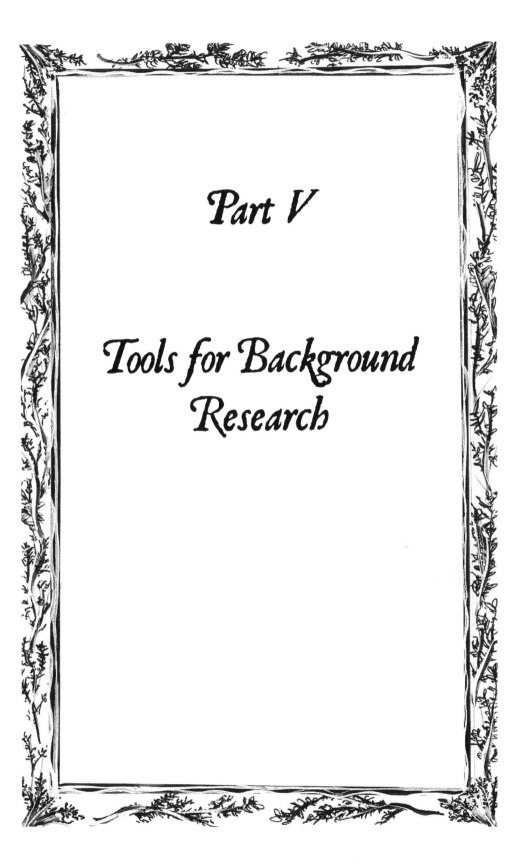

Part V

Tools for Background Research

Chapter 14

The Importance of Bibliographies

To recreate/redact historic recipes and understand what they reveal—either overtly or between the lines—you need reference materials, filled with sage advice and insights into the historical periods that interest you.

You might ask, "Why should I bother with bibliographies or other books? There's Google. That's all I need!"

True, Google is a wonder, and you'll find plenty of supportive material there (see Chapter 15). But much of what you need will come from sources that you cannot fully access through Google or the internet.

That's why coming up with a working bibliography is important.

However, compiling bibliographies is a bit like blowing bubbles, for you neither know how big the bubbles will be nor how far away they'll float through the air.

Or where they'll land.

And that's the exciting bit about bibliographies. You can't know when you set out on the journey where you'll end up.

One thing is for sure, and that's this: You'll need a working bibliography to support your quest to recreate historical recipes or analyze cookbooks from the past, or even the present.

If you compile bibliographies the old-fashioned way, without resorting to the sterility of database searching, the act itself often turns out to be more exciting than watching an episode of "Forensic Files." You may not stumble upon murder or mayhem—but you just might, if you read between the lines with the soul of a skeptic. One clue leads to another, until you're peering at a huge labyrinth of interlocking paths, all leading to the center, the core, the crux of your research.

The recipe for a good old-fashioned compilation starts with one basic ingredient: another bibliography, usually in a book highly regarded—that is, cited numerous times—by scholars or other experts in whatever endeavor you're undertaking.

Where the heck do you find this information?

One way is through a database search of such tools as the Web of Science, the old ISI Citation Indexes, or Elsevier's Scopus.[50]

Another, older way is to look at the bibliographies of several books on your topic. If the same books appear over and over, you've found your first clue.

From that, you can begin choosing references to look at from the bibliography of the most-cited book and go from there. The process resembles the creation of a large family tree. Hunting for information through a database can't compare to the thrill of running your finger down the page, checking off many references you most likely would never learn of while doing a database search.

Why?

Indexing is a process that doesn't always apply the same terms/tags where they should

be applied, given that humans do the initial applying. So, you might find references in your book that
won't turn up when you use your search terms in
the database.

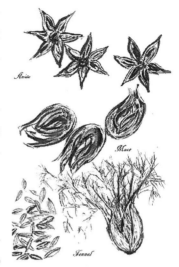

So when you begin to see the same references over and over again, you can be pretty sure
you've come face-to-face with the basic core bibliography of your topic.

What a joy!

As stated earlier, bibliographies stem from be-
ginnings akin to those of a family tree. They too
come to life with different physical characteristics. A simple definition of bibliography could be described as nothing more than "A list of books." [51] That's
just what you see at the back of most books and other works, an immensely
long list of books arranged by author's last name. Authors often label such
a bibliography as "Select Bibliography," implying that they perused many
other sources, but found those sources cited to be the most useful.

Bibliographies such as these, especially if they go on for pages and pages,
tend to be a bit useless for the serious researcher of whatever topic is under-
way. You can't tell whether or not a certain resource will provide anything
juicy for your pot, or paper/book/blog post, if you will. Unless you're willing
to check every single reference, scrutinizing bibliographies for pertinent references can be like panning for gilt nuggets in a cold rushing river: you need
to hurry and you might not strike gold, either.

But sometimes such a find crops up and you strike a vein of gold ore too good
to be true.

As a quick refresher on the process of creating bibliographies, and why it's
necessary, take a moment to read this clarification from 1916:

*A bibliography of a subject is to the literature of that subject what an index is to a book.
It shows the extent of that literature and the amount of work that has been bestowed*

upon it. It brings together scattered fragments of book knowledge and makes them readily accessible. Next to having knowledge is knowing where to go for it, and the only enduring guide in that direction is a bibliography.[52]

The most basic of bibliographies is the Enumerative or Subject Bibliography. A Subject Bibliography covers material about a particular subject and related topics. You'll find this type at the back of most books and other published material. It helps you, and your reader, to take the time to annotate the entries, which can be time-consuming. But arranging a bibliography by topic alone can be the next best thing if Father Time is not your friend. That's what you'll find in this book.

One of the most fascinating, and frustrating, aspects of bibliographies is that they're never complete. The poor bibliographer often views the bibliography in much the same way that Sisyphus must have while shoving that rock up the hill. Unending.

Chapter 15

Online Tools

Archaeology

Archaeological Studies of Cooking and Food Preparation: https://link.springer.com/article/10.1007/s10814-017-9111-5

An Anthropological Approach to Ancient Cooking Techniques: https://www.archaeology.wiki/blog/2012/10/30/an-anthropological-approach-to-ancient-cooking-techniques/

The Archaeologists and Chefs Recreating the World's Oldest Recipes: https://www.haaretz.com/archaeology/.premium.MAGAZINE-caviar-of-the-ancient-world-1.6071566

A Bibliography of Historical Archaeology in North America, North of Mexico (a bit dated): https://sha.org/resources/bibliographies/bha-north-america/s-z/

Organizations:

Society for Creative Anachronism: http://www.sca.org/

Society for Historical Archaeology: https://sha.org/

Society for American Archaeology: https://www.saa.org/

Art Databases

Catalogue of Digitized Medieval Manuscripts: https://digitizedmedievalmanuscripts.org/app/

Early American Images: https://jcb.lunaimaging.com/luna/servlet/JCB~1~1

The Fascination with Food in Art History: https://www.widewalls.ch/food-in-art-history/

Cookery Books - Digitized and Other Sources

Cookbooks in Digital Form: http://www.openculture.com/2016/07/an-archive-of-3000-vintage-cookbooks-lets-you-travel-back-through-culinary-time.html

https://gherkinstomatoes.com/online-cookbooks-sources/
(extensive list of many different sites)

Early Modern Culinary Texts—Digital: https://people.uwm.edu/
carlin/early-modern-culinary-texts-1500-1700/

Gallica (database from the BNF, National Library of France): https://
gallica.bnf.fr/

Handwritten Recipes Archive: http://www.openculture.com/2012/10/
archive_of_handwritten_recipes_1600_-_1960_will_teach_you_how_to_
stew_a_calfs_head_and_more.html

Household Books Published in Britain: 1475–1914: http://household-
books.ucdavis.edu/

Medieval Culinary Texts: https://people.uwm.edu/carlin/medieval-cu-
linary-texts-500-1500/

http://medievalcookery.com/etexts.html?England

Cooking the Basics - What You Need to Know

The Curious Cook: http://www.curiouscook.com/

Epicurious: https://www.epicurious.com/

Townsends 18th-Century Cooking: https://www.youtube.com/user/
jastownsendandson

Dictionaries

Anglo-Norman: http://www.anglo-norman.net/gate/

Catalan: www.catalandictionary.org/en/search

https://www.lexilogos.com/english/catalan_dictionary.htm

English:

Oxford English Dictionary: http://www.oed.com/

Bosworth-Toller Anglo-Saxon Dictionary: http://bosworth.ff.cuni.cz/

Middle English Dictionary: https://quod.lib.umich.edu/m/med/

Dictionary of Old English: https://tapor.library.utoronto.ca/doe/

Old English Translator: https://www.oldenglishtranslator.co.uk/

Lexilogos: https://www.lexilogos.com/english/english_old.htm

Middle English Compendium: https://quod.lib.umich.edu/m/mec/

French: https://sites01.lsu.edu/faculty/jgellri/sample-page/medieval-language-and-literature/medieval-french/

ARTFL Project: https://artfl-project.uchicago.edu/

Latin:

Perseus Latin Dictionary: http://www.perseus.tufts.edu/hopper/resolveform?redirect=true&lang=Latin

Spanish:

Diccionario de la lengua española: https://dle.rae.es/?w=diccionario

Resources for Medievalists in Hispanic Studies: https://libguides.bodleian.ox.ac.uk/hispanic-medieval

El corpus del español: http://www.corpusdelespanol.org/

Tentative Dictionary of Medieval Spanish: https://babel.hathitrust.org/cgi/pt?id=mdp.39015005722783;view=1up;seq=7

Document and Title Page Analysis

Analyzing an Historical Document: http://faculty.marianopolis.edu/c.belanger/quebechistory/Howtoanalyzeanhistoricaldocument.html

Sample analysis form: http://www.eiu.edu/eiutps/Final_Historical%20Document_Kerri.pdf

Title Pages: https://rbscp.lib.rochester.edu/2441

Equipment and Material Culture

Brewing Tools: https://www.probrewer.com/tools/

Colonial-Era Pottery Identification: https://homeguides.sfgate.com/identify-colonialera-pottery-100142.html

History of Household Technology: http://www.loc.gov/rr/scitech/tracer-bullets/householdtb.html

The Kitchen: http://www.tcnj.edu/~anchouse/kitchen.html

Kitchen Antiques: http://www.oldandinteresting.com/kitchen-antiques.aspx

Renaissance Kitchen Equipment: http://www.katjaorlova.com/MedievalKitchenEquipment.htm

Food History - General

Historic Food—Ivan Day's Site: www.historicfood.com

"How to Do Food History," by Rachel Laudan: http://www.rachellaudan.com/getting-started-in-food-history

Oxford Food Symposium Proceedings/Downloads: https://www.
oxfordsymposium.org.uk/proceedings/downloads/

Food Safety and Quantity Cooking

ALHFAM Food Safety Manual: https://www.alhfam.org/resources/
Documents/PIGS/Food/ALHFAM%20Food%20Safety%20Manual-2-16.
pdf

Chef Menu Food Quantity Chart: https://www.chef-menus.com/
food-quantity-chart.html

Cooking for Groups: A Volunteer's Guide to Food Safety: https://
www.fsis.usda.gov/wps/portal/fsis/topics/food-safety-education/
get-answers/food-safety-fact-sheets/safe-food-handling/cooking-for-
groups-a-volunteers-guide-to-food-safety

Food Quantities for 100: http://www.ellenskitchen.com/bigpots/plan/
quan100.html

Glossaries

Glossaries of Historic Cookery Terms: http://www.angelfire.com/
md3/openhearthcooking/aaGlossaries-time-measure.html

Glossary of Medieval Cookery Terms: http://www.godecookery.com/
glossary/glossary.htm

Ingredients

Columbian Exchange: https://scholar.harvard.edu/files/nunn/files/
nunn_qian_jep_2010.pdf

https://dcc.newberry.org/collections/foods-of-the-columbian-exchange

Herbs and Spices of the Middle Ages—A Booklist: http://www.gal-
lowglass.org/jadwiga/herbs/herbbooks.html

Ingredient Weight Chart: https://www.kingarthurflour.com/learn/
ingredient-weight-chart.html

Libraries Containing Culinary History Collections

Advice on Traveling to Libraries: http://www.fordham.edu/halsall/
byz/mssacc.html

Beinecke Rare Book and Manuscript Library: https://beinecke.library.
yale.edu/

Bibliothèque nationale de France: http://www.bnf.fr/fr/acc/x.accueil.
html

Bodleian Library, Oxford: https://www.bodleian.ox.ac.uk/

British Library: https://www.bl.uk/

Cambridge University Library: http://www.lib.cam.ac.uk/

Harvard University Libraries: https://library.harvard.edu/

Hill Museum and Manuscript Library: http://hmml.org/

Huntington Library: http://www.huntington.org/

Medieval Institute Library, University of Notre Dame: https://library.nd.edu/medieval/

National Library of Scotland: https://www.nls.uk/

Pierpont Morgan Library: https://www.themorgan.org/

Princeton University Libraries: http://library.princeton.edu/

The Schøyen Collection: https://www.schoyencollection.com/

University of Pennsylvania Rare Book and Manuscript Library: http://www.library.upenn.edu/kislak

Literacy - European History
https://cookbookhistory.wordpress.com/
(Scroll down to section "The Literate, the Semi-Literate, and the Hungry")

Measurements, Weights, and Money
Currency Exchanges and Prices, Medieval: http://www2.scc.rutgers.edu/memdb/aboutmemdb.html

Dictionary of Units and Measures: http://www.ibiblio.org/units/

Measuring Worth, The British Pound Since 1270: https://www.measuringworth.com/calculators/ppoweruk/

Medieval Crop Yields Database, 1211–1491: http://www.cropyields.ac.uk/index.php

Roman Numerals Converter: https://www.thecalculatorsite.com/misc/romannumerals.php

Medicinal Recipes
Folger Shakespeare Library: https://folgerpedia.folger.edu/Beyond_Home_Remedy:_Women,_Medicine,_and_Science

National Library of Medicine: https://circulatingnow.nlm.nih.gov/2017/04/13/digitizing-material-culture-handwritten-recipe-books-1600-1900/

Menu Collections

Menus for Feasts, 1387 and 1443: http://sites.fas.harvard.edu/~chaucer/special/lifemann/manners/feast.html

Menus from Medieval Sources: http://medievalcookery.com/menus/menus.html

Vintage Menus: https://www.gjenvick.com/VintageMenus/index.html

Paleography and Writing

Abbreviations in Scribal Writing: https://en.wikipedia.org/wiki/Scribal_abbreviation

https://kuscholarworks.ku.edu/bitstream/handle/1808/1821/47cappelli.pdf

https://www.ruhr-uni-bochum.de/philosophy/projects/abbreviationes/index.html

Medieval Writing (examples and explanations): http://medievalwriting.50megs.com/scripts/scrindex.htm

Reading Old Handwriting: http://researchguides.library.vanderbilt.edu/HIST3000W-Blackett/handwriting

Simple Explanation of the Correct Usage of the Long and Short S with the Addition of Examples for the Ease of Use: https://imgur.com/gallery/0sVAa

Spanish Abbreviations: https://script.byu.edu/Pages/Spanish/en/chabbreviations.aspx

Timelines and Calendars

The Medieval Year: http://users.telenet.be/willy.vancammeren/NBC/nbc_medieval_year.htm

Timeline of Social History, Manners, and Menus: http://www.food-timeline.org/food1.html

Timeline of Western Cookbooks: https://cookbookhistory.wordpress.com/timeline-of-western-cookbooks/

Chapter 16

A Final Word

You can never be 100 percent certain that people cooked the recipes you find in historic cookbooks. Nor can you always be sure they ate the food, either! But you can look at cookbooks as one more useful tool in clarifying the historical record, even in historical archaeology. Clues and hints reveal themselves in myriad ways, through close readings of the texts, awareness of past trends in cookery and its history, and knowledge of cooking techniques. Cookbooks may serve as nostalgic mementos for people far from their cultural or national origins, facing deprivation that forced them to eat purslane and other foods viewed as famine foods.

On the other hand, cookbooks provide a window into the kitchen, a place that historically has generated little documentation, due to it being considered women's domain. Or the domain of people whom society found questionable. Recreating historic recipes with today's ingredients and equipment results in a taste of bygone times, creating a sort of kinship with those who went before us, by tying together past, present, and future.

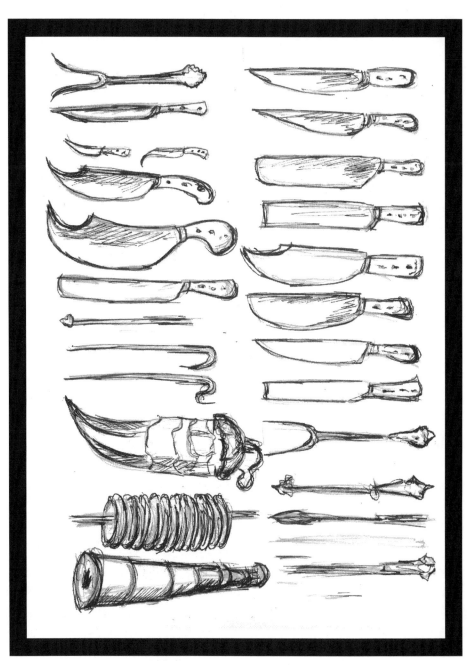

Endnotes

1. Cynthia D. Bertelsen, "Daily Life Through Cooking and Cookbooks: A Brief Guide to Using Cookbooks as a Tool in Historical Archaeology," *Artifact* 49 (2011): 1-26.

2. Kristine Kowalchuk, ed. *Preserving on Paper: Seventeenth-Century Englishwomen's Receipt Books* (Toronto: University of Toronto Press, 2017) 11.

3. France and Italy contributed a great deal to culinary history, and not just in Europe. For France, see Barbara Ketchum Wheaton's *Savoring the Past: The French Kitchen and Table from 1300-1789* (1983) and D. Eleanor Scully's and Terence Scully's *Early French Cookery: Sources, History, Original Recipes and Modern Adaptations* (1995). For Italy, see Alberto Cappatti's and Massimo Montinari's *Italian Cuisine: A Cultural History* (2003).

4. In some editions, the title pages read "Motiño," while others convey the name as "Montiño." Spanish culinary history expert, Carolyn Nadeau, gives the name as "Montiño," so I follow her lead here.

5. Kowalchuk, 19.

6. Information from the records of the Virginia Company: "Markhams and Goouges booke of all kynd of English husbandry and huswifry, and 2 others for the orderinge of silk and silkwormes are nowe sent, wch take into your owne hands from Thomas Lemis, otherwise you will bee defrauded of them." *CXXXVIII. Richard Berkeley and John Smyth. A Commission to George Thorpe for the Government of the Plantation September 10, 1620*

Smyth of Nibley Papers, Smyth, 3 (26), Pages 129–131 Document in New York Public Library List of Records No. 206

Endnotes

7. E. Smith—some scholars are not certain that the author's name was Eliza, as is commonly believed.

8. Henry Notaker, *A History of Cookbooks: From Kitchen to Page over Seven Centuries* (Berkeley: University of California Press, 2017) 65.

9. You might say that cooking is any human manipulation of foodstuff. Consider ceviche. Oysters on ice?

10. See **Cookbooks as Historical Resources** section in **Selected Bibliographical Resources**.

11. Guilds emerged during the Middle Ages, specifically 1170 A.D. in England, and were either merchant- or craft-oriented, including bakers. The word "guild" comes from the Saxon word "gilden," meaning "to pay." Guilds were similar to modern-day labor unions.

12. See Terence Scully's publications for more on French culinary history.

13. See **Historiography and Historical Theory** section in **Selected Bibliographical Resources**.

14. Elizabeth M. Scott, " 'A Little Gravy in the Dish and Onions in a Tea Cup': What Cookbooks Reveal About Material Culture." *International Journal of Historical Archaeology* 1(2) (1997): 153.

15. Scully, 4.

16. See Robert A. Houston, *Literacy in Early Modern Europe, 1500-1800* (New York: Routledge, 2016) and David Cressy, *Literacy and the Social Order: Reading and Writing in Tudor and Stuart England* (Cambrigde: Cambridge University Press, 2009). His numbers suggest that, in the 1500s, 90 percent of men and 99 percent of women were illiterate. Thomas More wrote about literacy in England in 1533:

http://www.thomasmorestudies.org/1557Workes/Apology1.pdf

17. See definition of plagiarism, page 30.

18. Rippmann, Dorothee. " 'Take almaundes blaunched …' Cookbooks in the Middle Ages and Early Modern Times." Ed. Johannes Grabmeyer. *Culinary Art: History and Marketing.* 76.

19. Hippocrates (c. 460–c. 377 B.C.) was a Greek physician, known as the "Father of Medicine." Galen (A.D. 129—c.199) practiced medicine in Greece as well. Over 100 pieces of his writing still exist. He supported the concept of the four humors and his teaching influenced Western medicine for centuries.

20. Platina. *De Honesta voluptate et valetudine* (On Right Pleasure and Good Health). (Ed. and Trans. Mary Ella Millham. Tempe, Az: Medieval & Renaissance Texts & Studies, 1998) 117.

21. *Martha Washington's Booke of Cookery.* (Ed. Karen Hess. New York: Columbia University Press, 1995) 206.

22. http://lavarenne.com/2013/12/limited-edition-the-cookbook-tree-of-life-broadside-print-is-here/

23. Quote attributed to Dr. Samuel Johnson. See page 80 of *The London Quarterly Review*, volume 54-55, July 1835. In a review of Louis Eustache Ude's *French Cook*, there's a reference to John Wilson Croker's *Boswell*, volume iv, page 43, 1831: " 'You shall see what a book of cookery I shall make'—said Dr. Johnson, and the reader will not fail to observe that this is the fourth time we have been enabled to appeal to him as an authority—'Women can spin very well, but they cannot write a good book of cookery.' I could write a better book of cookery than has ever yet been written ; it should be a book on philosophical principles."

24. Sarah Peters Kernan. 'For al them that delight in Cookery': The Production and Use of Cookery Books in England, 1300–1600. (PhD dissertation. The Ohio State University, 2016) 26. Kernan refutes Stephen Mennell's statements that early scrolls and other cookery manuscripts were not used in kitchens (Mennell, 1985, 87).

25. The Catholic Monarchs—Isabella la Católica (A.D. 151-1504), Queen of Castile, and Ferdinand of Aragon (A.D. 1452-1516)—reunited Spain, expelled

the Moors and Jews, and funded Christopher Columbus's New World voyages.

26. Sandra Sherman. *Invention of the Modern Cookbook*. (Denver: Greenwood Press, 2010) 40.

27. Kernan, 5-6.

28. Based on a 1675 quote from Sir Isaac Newton, the discoverer of gravitational theory: "If I have seen further, it is by standing on the shoulders of Giants."

29. Hilary Spurling. *Elinor Fettiplace's Receipt Book: Elizabethan Country House Cooking*. (London. Penguin Books, 1986).

30. *Martha Washington's Booke of Cookery*, 5.

31. Perry, *Anonymous Andalusian*.

32. See Rachel Laudan. "The Mexican Kitchen's Islamic Connections." *Saudi Aramco World*, 2004, 32-39. and Toby Peterson. "The Arab Influence on Western European Cooking." *Journal of Medieval History* 6: 317-340, 1980.

33. See Rhonda M. Gonzales, "The African Presence in New Spain, c. 1528-1700" (excellent bibliography)

http://www.pvamu.edu/tiphc/research-projects/afro-mexicans-afro-mestizos/the-african-presence-in-new-spain-c-1528-1700/

34. Ruperto de Nola also known as Mestre Robert.

35. See section **Historiography and Historical Theory** in **Selected Bibliographical Resources**.

36. Exceptions include the work of Cristina Barros, Lourdes Ortiz-Díaz, Vicky Hayward, and Igor Cusack.

37. A *chinois* is a conical-shaped mesh sieve found in French *batteries de cuisine*.

38. Basic medieval sauces included Cameline, Mustard, Jance, Yellow

Pepper, and Black Pepper.

39. Cookstoves evolved over the centuries, from hearths to ceramic to iron to electric and gas. Various inventors tinkered with designs, including an American woman, Mary Evard, awarded a patent in 1850 for her invention of the Reliance Cook Stove.

40. Lennox Hastie. *Finding Fire: Cooking at its Most Elemental.* (London: Hardie Grant Books, 2017) 42.

41. Hastie, 43.

42. Nancy Carter Crump. *Hearthside Cooking: Early American Southern Cuisine Updated for Today's Hearth & Cookstove.* 2nd edition. Chapel Hill: University of North Carolina Press, 2008) 16.

43. Verjus/verjuice is made from the acidic juice of unripened grapes. Vinegar maybe substituted.

44. Gervase Markham. *The English Housewife, Containing the inward and outward virtues which ought to be in a complete woman ... .* (Ed. Michael Best. Montreal: McGill-Queen's University Press, 1986) 8.

45. A pipkin is an earthenware pot/pan.

46. The Star Court was an English court of law, a room with a star-studded ceiling.

47. The Worshipful Company of Cooks began as a London guild for cooks in the twelfth century. It still exists. See Alan Borg's *A History of the Worshipful Company of Cooks.* London: Jeremy Mills Publishing Ltd., 2011.

48. Robert May, *The Accomplisht Cook, or the Art and Mystery of Cookery.* (Ed. Alan Davidson. Blackawton, Totnes, Devon, U.K.: Prospect Books, 2012) preface, n.p., paragraph 1.

49. M.P. refers to "member of Parliament."

50. Web of Science: https://clarivate.com/products/web-of-science/

Endnotes

ISI Citation Indexes: https://www.utoledo.edu/library/help/guides/docs/ISIcitation.pdf

Elsevier's Scopus: https://www.elsevier.com/solutions/scopus

51. Roy Stokes, *The Function of Bibliography.* 2nd edition. (Aldershot: Gower Publishing Co. Ltd., 1982) 1.

52. Louis Nicholas Feipel, *Elements of Bibliography.* (Chicago: University of Chicago Press, 1916) 31.

Appendix

Ingredients and Flavorings

Recipe Reconstruction Form

Flavorings Available in Western Europe Prior to 1492

Anise	Galingale	Oregano
Asafoetida	Garlic	Parsley
Basil	Ginger	Pennyroyal
Betony	Grains of	Purslane
Black Pepper	Paradise	Ramson
Borage	Honey	Red sage
Caraway	Horseradish	Rosemary
Cardamom	Hyssop	Rosewater
Celery	Lavender	Rue
Chervil	Lemon	Saffron
Chickweed	Liquamen	Sage
Chicory	Long Pepper	Samphire
Chives	Lovage	Sandalwood
Cilantro	Mace	Savory
Cinnamon	Marjoram	Silphium
Clary	Mastic	Southernwood
Cloves	Mint	Spearmint
Coriander	Musk	Spikenard
Costmary	Mustard	Sugar
Cubeb Pepper	Mustard	Sumac
Cumin	Nettles	Tansy
Dill	Nutmeg	Tarragon
Fennel	Orach	Thyme
Fenugreek	Orange	Turnsole

Flavorings Available in Western Europe After 1492*

Allspice

Cayenne Pepper

Paprika

Turmeric

Vanilla

*In addition to those listed above.

Appendix

Vegetables, Nuts, and Legumes Available in Western Europe

PRIOR TO 1492		AFTER 1492	OTHER/LATER
Acorn	Laver	Bell Pepper	Broccoli
Almond	Leek	Cashew	Brussels
Arugula	Lentil	Coconut	Sprouts
Alexander	Lettuce	Corn	Kohlrabi
Artichoke	Mushroom	Jerusalem	Rutabaga
Asparagus	Olive	Artichoke	
Beet	Onion	Kidney	
Cabbage	Orach	beans	
Carrot	Parsnip	Pecan	
Cauliflower	Pea	Potato	
Celery	Radish	Pumpkin	
Chard	Rocket	Red Pepper	
Chestnut	Salsify	String bean	
Chickpea	Sesame	Sweet	
Cress	Seed	Potato	
Cucumber	Shallot	Squash	
Eggplant	Skirret	Sunflower	
Endive	Spinach	Seeds	
Eringo roots	Turnip	Yam	
Fava bean	Walnut		
Filbert	Watercress		
Garlic			
Gourd			

Protein Sources In Western Europe

Pre-1492	Added After 1492
Cheese: soft and hard, such as grana, Roquefort, Ricotta, curds, whey, Manchego	Turkey
	Pacific Salmon
Butter: from cow, sheep, goat	
Eggs: duck, chicken, goose	
Pork	
Rabbit	
Beef and Veal	
Game: Venison, Hare, Wild Fowl	
Fish and Shellfish: Oysters, Shrimp, Mussels, Crayfish	
Fowl: Chickens, Capons, Pullets, Geese, Ducks, Swans, Pheasants, Peacocks, Doves, Pigeons, Partridges, Quail, Woodcocks	

Step-By-Step Recipe Reconstruction Form

1. Recipe name and source:

_____

_____

_____

2. Original recipe. Check for similar recipes in other sources, if possible. Include translation and transliterations as well.

_____

_____

_____

3. Ingredients in original recipe:

_____

_____

_____

_____

_____

_____

4. Equipment, procedures required, action words

_____

_____

_____

_____

5. Unclear words and language:

_____

_____

_____

6. Resources used to clarify wordage, procedure, other issues:

_____

_____

_____

_____

7. Notes regarding the final dish, what you would redo, change:

_____

_____

_____

_____

8. Modern version of the recipe:

_____

_____

_____

_____

_____

_____

_____

_____

_____

_____

_____

_____

_____

_____

_____

_____

_____

_____

_____

_____

_____

_____

Selected Bibliographical Resources

Primary Sources

A number of the following are translations or transcriptions.

Arabic:

al-Warraq, Ibn Sayyer. *Annals of the Caliphs' Kitchens: Ibn Sayyar al-Warraq's Tenth-century Baghdadi Cookbook (Kitab al-Tabikh [The Book of Dishes])*. Ed. and Trans. Nawal Nasrallah. York: E. J. Brill, 2007. (From a 10th-century manuscript.)

Catalan (see also Spanish):

The Book of Sent Soví: Medieval Recipes from Catalonia. Ed. Joan Santanach. Barcelona: Barcino-Tamesis, 2008. (From a fourteenth-century manuscript.)

English:

A. W. *A Booke of Cookrye*. London: Edward Allde. 1591.

Boorde, Andrew. *The Breviary of Healthe*. London: W. Powell. 1547.

_____. *Hereafter foloweth a compendyous regyment or a dyetary of helth: made in Mou[n]tpyllier, compyled by Andrew Boorde of physiycke doctour, dedycated to the armypotent prynce, and valyaunt Lorde Thomas Duke of Northfolche*. London: Robert Wyer, 1542.

Digby, Kenelm. *The Closet Of Sir Kenelm Digby Knight, Opened*. London: Brome, 1669.

Evelyn, John. *Acetaria: A Discourse of Sallets*. London: B. Tooke, 1699.

The Forme of Cury. Ed. Samuel Pegge. J. Nichols: London, 1780.

Giegher, Matthias. *Li tre trattati*. Padova: Guaresco Guareschi al Pozzo dipinto, 1629.

Glasse, Hannah. *"First Catch Your Hare ...": The Art of Cookery, Made Plain and Easy, by a Lady*. Blackawton, Totnes, Devon, U.K.: Prospect Books, 2012. (Facsimile of 1747 first edition)

Hieatt, Constance B. and Sharon Butler. *Curye on Inglysch: English Culinary Manuscripts of the Fourteenth Century (Including the Forme of Curye)*. London: Early English Text Society, 1985.

Hieatt, Constance F. and Robin F. Jones. "Two Anglo-Norman Culinary Collections Edited from British Library Manuscripts Additional 32085 and Royal 12.C.xii." Speculum. 61 (4): 859-882, October 1986.

Markham, Gervase. *The English Housewife, Containing the inward and outward virtues which ought to be in a complete woman … .* Ed. Michael Best. Montreal: McGill-Queen's University Press, 1986. (Transcription of 1615 edition.)

May, Robert. *The Accomplisht Cook, or the Art and Mystery of Cookery.* Ed. Alan Davidson. Blackawton, Totnes, Devon, U.K.: Prospect Books, 2012. (Facsimile of 1685 edition.)

Murrell, John. *Murrells Two Bookes of Cookerie and Carving.* London: M. Flesher for John Marriot, 1631.

A Noble Boke off Cookry ffor a Prynce Houssolde or eny other Estately Houssolde. Ed. Robina Napier. Reprinted Verbatim from a Rare MS. in the Holkham Collection. London: Elliot Stock, 1882.

A Proper Newe Booke of Cookery. London: Richard Lant and Richard Bankes, 1545. See also A Proper Newe Booke of Cokerye: Margaret Parker's Cookery Book. Ed. Anne Ahmed. Cambridge: Corpus Christie College, 2002.

Randolph, Mary. *The Virgina House-wife.* Ed. Karen Hess. Columbia: University of South Carolina Press, 1984.

Smith, E. *The Compleat Housewife: or, Accomplish'd Gentlewoman's Companion.* London: J. Pemberton, 1727.

Woolley, Hannah. *The Queen-Like Closet.* London: Richard Lowndes, 1672.

_____. *The Gentlewomans Companion or, A Guide to the Female Sex.* London: Dorman Newman, 1673.

French:
La Varenne's Cookery: The French Cook; The French Pastry Chef; The French Confectioner. Ed. and Trans. Terence Scully. Blackawton, Totnes, Devon, U.K.: Prospect Books, 2006.

Italian:
L'Arte et prudenze d'un maestro Cuoco (The Opera of Bartolmeo Scappi 1570). Ed. and Trans. Terence Scully. Toronto: University of Toronto Press, 2008.

Ballerini, Luigi, ed. *The Art of Cooking: The First Modern Cookery Book.* Ed. and Trans. Jeremey Parzen. Berkeley: University of California Press, 2005. (With fifty modernized recipes by Stefania Barzini.)

Cuoco Napoletano (The Neapolitan Recipe Collection). Ed. and Trans. Terence Scully. Ann Arbor: University of Michigan Press, 2000.

Selected Bibliographical Resources

Giegher, Matthias. *Li tre trattati*. Padua: Guaresco Guareschi al Pozzo dipinto, 1639.

Platina. *De Honesta voluptate et valetudine* (On Right Pleasure and Good Health). Ed. and Trans. Mary Ella Millham. Tempe, Ariz.: Medieval & Renaissance Texts & Studies, 1998.

Scappi, Bartolomeo. *The Opera of Bartolomeo Scappi*. Ed. and Trans. Terence Scully. Toronto: University of Toronto Press, 2008. (Original printing 1570.)

Spanish:

Altamiras, Juan. *Nuevo arte de cocina, sacado de la escuela de la experiencia economica.* Madrid: Antonio Perez de Soto, a expensas de Don Pedro Joseph Alonso y Padilla. 1760. Spanish text online: https://www.zaragoza.es/contenidos/museos/arte-cocina-altamiras.pdf

Anonymous Anadalusian. Trans. Charles Perry. http://www.daviddfriedman.com/Medieval/Cookbooks/Andalusian/andalusian_footnotes.htm

http://www.daviddfriedman.com/Medieval/Cookbooks/Andalusian/andalusian_contents.htm

Cabeza de Vaca Gilbert, Fabiola. *The Good Life: New Mexico Traditions and Food*. Santa Fe: Museum of New Mexico Press, 1982.

Hernández de Maceras, Domingo. *Libro del Arte de Cozina*. Salamanca: Antonia Ramirez, 1607.

Jaramillo, Cleofas. *The Genuine Tasty New Mexico Recipes*. Santa Fe: Seton Village Press, 1939.

Libro de cocina del hermano fray Gerónimo de San Pelayo, Mexico, siglo XVIII. Ed. Teresa Castello Yturbide. Mexico: CONACULTA, 2003.

Llibre de totes maneres de confits. Boletín de la Real Academia de Buenas Letras de Barcelona 19: 97-134, 1946. (From a 14th-century manuscript.)

Manual de mugeres en el cual se contienen muchas y diversas recetas muy buenas. Ed. Alicia Martínez Crespo. Ediciones Universidad Salamanca: Salamanca, 1995. (From a 16th-century manuscript.)

Montiño Martínez, Francisco. *Arte de cocina, pastelería, bizcochería y conservería*. Madrid: Luis Sanchez, 1611.

Nola, Ruperto de. *Libro de guisados, manjares y potaje*. Companía Ibero-Americana de Publicaciones, Madrid. 1929. (From a 1525 manuscript and the original Catalan version, *Libre del coch*)

http://allandalus.com/apicius/Libro%20de%20guisados%20Ruperto%20Nola.pdf

Tipton, Alice Stevens. *New Mexico Cookery: Some Products of the State and How to Prepare Them.* Santa Fe: State Land Office, 1916.

Secondary Sources

Archaeology:

Gifford-Gonzalez, Diane and Kojun Ueno Sunseri. "Foodways on the Frontier: Animal Use and Identity in Early Colonial New Mexico". Ed. Kathryn C. Twiss. *The Archaeology of Food and Identity*, Center for Archaeological Investigations Occasional Paper No. 34. Southern Illinois University, Carbondale, Illinois, 2007, 260-285.

Graff, Sarah R. and Enrique Rodríguez-Alegría. *The Menial Art of Cooking: Archaeological Studies of Cooking and Food Preparation.* Boulder: University Press of Colorado, 2012.

Gray, Annie. " 'A Practical Art': an archaeological perspective on the use of recipe books." Eds. Michelle DiMeo and Sara Pennell. *Reading and Writing Recipe Books, 1550-1810.* Manchester: Manchester University Press, 2013.

Hastorf, Christine A. *The Social Archaeology of Food: Thinking about Eating from Prehistory to the Present.* Cambridge: Cambridge University Press, 2018.

Hume, Audrey Noel. *Food.* Williamsburg, VA: Colonial Williamsburg Foundation, 1978.

Larsen, Clark Spencer. *Bioarchaeology: Interpreting Behavior from the Human Skeleton.* 2nd edition. Cambridge: Cambridge University Press, 2015.

Metheny, Karen Bescherera and Mary C. Beaudry, eds. *Archaeology of Food: An Encyclopedia.* Lanham, Md.: Rowman & Littlefield, 2015.

Nottingham PG Conference. *Food & Drink in Archaeology 4.* Blackawton, Totnes, Devon, U.K.: Prospect Books, 2015.

Scott, Elizabeth M. " 'A Little Gravy in the Dish and Onions in a Tea Cup': What Cookbooks Reveal About Material Culture." *International Journal of Historical Archaeology* 1(2): 131-155, 1997.

Vroom, Joanit et al., eds. *Medieval Masterchef: Archaeological and Historical Perspectives on Eastern Cuisine and Western Foodways.* Turnhout, Belgium: Brepols Publishers N.V., 2017.

Woolgar, C. M. et al. *Food in Medieval England: Diet and Nutrition.* Oxford: Oxford University Press, 2006.

Cookbooks, Cooking, and the Science of Cookery: The Basics

Allen, Darina. *Forgotten Skills of Cooking.* London: Kyle Books, 2009.

Andrews, Coleman. *Catalan Cuisine: Europe's Last Great Culinary Secret.* Cambridge: Harvard Common Press, 1999.

Barrow, Cathy. *Mrs. Wheelbarrow's Practical Pantry: Recipes and Techniques for Year-Round Preserving.* New York: W. W. Norton & Company, 2014.

Cunningham, Marion. *The Fannie Farmer Cookbook: A Tradition of Good Cooking for a New Generation of Cooks.* New York: Bantam. 1994.

Davison, Jan. *English Sausages.* Blackawton, Totnes, Devon, U.K.: Prospect Books, 2015.

Grigson, Jane. *The Art of Making Sausages, Pâtés, and Other Charcuterie.* New York: Alfred A. Knopf, 1983.

_____. *English Food.* London: Penguin Books, 1974.

Katz, Sandor Ellix. *The Art of Fermentation: An In-depth Exploration of Essential Concepts and Processes from Around the World.* White River Junction, Vt.: Chelsea Green Publishing, 2012.

Larousse Gastronomique: The Encyclopedia of Food, Wine and Cookery. New York: Crown Publishers, 1961.

McGee, Harold. *On Food and Cooking: The Science and Lore of the Kitchen.* Revised edition. New York: Scribner, 2004.

Peterson, James. *Cooking: 600 Recipes, 1500 Photographs,* One Kitchen Education. Berkeley: Ten Speed Press, 2007.

_____. *Essentials of Cooking.* New York: Artisan, 1999.

Roden, Claudia. *The Food of Spain.* New York: Ecco, 2011.

Rombauer, Irma S. and Becker, Marion Rombauer. *Joy of Cooking.* New York: Bobbs Merrill, 1964.

Rozin, Elizabeth. *Ethnic Cuisine: How to Create the Authentic Flavors of Over 30 International Cuisines.* London: Penguin Books, 1992.

Ruhlman, Michael. *Ratio: The Simple Codes Behind the Craft of Everyday Cooking.* New York: Simon & Schuster, 2010.

_____. *The Elements of Cooking: Translating the Chef's Craft for Every Kitchen.* New York: Scribner, 2010.

Cookbooks of Recreated ("Redacted") Recipes:

Altamiras, Juan. *Art of Cookery: A Spanish Friar's Kitchen Notebook.* Ed. Vicky Hayward. Lanham, Md.: Rowman & Littlefield, 2017.

Black, Maggie. *The Medieval Cookbook.* Revised edition. Los Angeles: J. Paul Getty Museum, 2012.

Blumenthal, Heston. *Historic Heston.* London: Bloomsbury, 2014.

Brears, Peter. *All the King's Cooks: The Tudor Kitchens of King Henry VIII at Hampton Court Palace.* London: Souvenir Press, 1999.

_____. *Cooking & Dining in Medieval England.* Blackawton, Totnes, Devon, U.K.: Prospect Books, 2008.

_____. *Cooking & Dining in Tudor & Early Stuart England.* Blackawton, Totnes, Devon, U.K.: Prospect Books, 2015.

Butler, Sharon. *Pleyn Delit: Medieval Cookery for Modern Cooks.* Toronto: University of Toronto Press, 1996.

Crump, Nancy Carter. *Hearthside Cooking: Early American Southern Cuisine Updated for Today's Hearth & Cookstove.* 2nd edition. Chapel Hill: University of North Carolina Press, 2008.

Friedman, David and Cook, Elizabeth. *A Miscellany.* CreateSpace, 2011.

Redon, Odile, et al. *The Medieval Kitchen: Recipes from France and Italy.* Chicago: University of Chicago Press, 1988.

Sass, Lorna. *To the King's Taste: Elizabethan Feasts and Recipes.* New York: Metropolitan Museum of Art, 1975.

_____. *To the Queen's Taste: Richard II's Book of Feasts and Recipes.* New York: Metropolitan Museum of Art, 1976.

Spurling, Hilary. *Elinor Fettiplace's Receipt Book: Elizabethan Country House Cooking.* London: Penguin Books, 1986.

Cookbooks as Historical Resources:

Albala, Ken. "Cookbooks as Historical Documents." *The Oxford Handbook of Food History*. Ed. Jeffrey Pilcher. Oxford: Oxford University Press, 2012, 227-240.

_____. "Cooking as Research Methodology." *Renaissance Food from Rabelais to Shakespeare: Culinary Readings and Culinary Histories*. Ed. Joan Fitzpatrick. Farnham: Ashgate, 2010, 73-88.

Appadurai, Arjun. "How to Make a National Cuisine: Cookbooks in Contemporary India." *Comparative Studies in Society and History* 30(1): 3-24, 1988.

Bak-Geller Corona, Sarah. "*Los recetarios 'afrancesados' del siglo XIX en México. La construcción de la nación mexicana y de un modelo culinario nacional.*" *Anthropology of Food*, 2009. https://journals.openedition.org/aof/6465

Barros, Cristina. *Los Libros de la Cocina Mexicana*. Mexico: CONACULTA, 2008.

Beck, Leonard N. "Praise Is Due Bartolomeo Platina: A Note on the Librarian-Author of the First Cookbook." *The Quarterly Journal of the Library of Congress* 32 (3): 238–253, 1975.

Bertelsen, Cynthia D. "Daily Life Through Cooking and Cookbooks: A Brief Guide to Using Cookbooks as a Tool in Historical Archaeology," *Artifact* 49: 1-26, 2011.

Davidson, Alan. "The Natural History of British Cookery Books." *The American Scholar* 52 (1): 98–106, 1983.

DiMeo, Michelle and Pennell, Sara, eds. *Reading and Writing Recipe Books, 1550-1800*. Manchester: Manchester University Press, 2013.

Foote, Cheryl. "Chile, Frijoles, and Bizcochitos: Recording, Preserving, and Promoting New Mexico's Culinary Heritage, 1890-1940." *Sunshine and Shadows in New Mexico's Past: The Statehood Period*. Vol. 3. Ed. Richard Melzer. Los Ranchos, N.M.: Rio Grande Books, 2012. n.p.

Hazlitt, W. C. *Old Cookery Books and Ancient Cuisine*. London, 1902.

Hieatt, Constance B. *Concordance of English Recipes: Thirteenth Through Fifteenth Centuries*. Tempe, Az: Arizona Center for Medieval and Renaissance Studies, 2006.

Humble, Nicola. *Culinary Pleasures: Cookbooks and the Transformation of British Food*. London: Faber and Faber, 2005.

Jaine, Tom. "Do Cookery Books Tell the Truth?" *Culinary History*. Eds. Lynn Martin and Barbara Santich. Brompton: East Street Publications, 2004, 87-96.

Jenkins, Nancy Harmon. "Two Ways of Looking at Maestro Martino." *Gastronomica* 7 (2): 97-103, 2007.

Kernan, Sarah Peters. '*For al them that delight in Cookery': The Production and Use of Cookery Books in England, 1300–1600.* PhD dissertation. The Ohio State University, 2016.

Kowalchuk, Kristine, ed. *Preserving on Paper: Seventh-Century Englishwomen's Receipt Books.* Toronto: University of Toronto Press, 2017.

Lehman, Gillian. *The British Housewife: Cookery Books, Cooking, and Society in Eighteenth-Century Britain.* Blackawton, Totnes, Devon, U.K.: Prospect Books, 2003.

Maclean, Virginia. *A Short-title Catalogue of Household and Cookery Books Published in the English Tongue 1701-1800.* London: Prospect Books, 1981.

Mac Con Iomaire, Maírtín. "Towards a Structured Approach to Reading Historic Cookbooks." *M/C Journal* 16 (3), 2013. Available at: <http://journal.media-culture.org.au/index.php/mcjournal/article/view/649>.

Notaker, Henry. *A History of Cookbooks: From Kitchen to Page over Seven Centuries.* Berkeley: University of California Press, 2017.

Nussel, Jill. "Heating Up the Sources: Using Community Cookbooks in Historical Inquiry." *History Compass* 4/5: 956-961, 2006.

Oxford, Arthur Whitaker. *English Cookery Books to Year 1850.* London: Henry Frowde, 1913.

Pennell, Sara. *The Birth of the English Kitchen, 1600 – 1850.* London: Bloomsbury, 2016.

Peterson, Toby. "The Arab Influence on Western European Cooking." *Journal of Medieval History* 6: 317-340, 1980.

Rodinson, Maxime. "Studies in Arabic Manuscripts Related to Cookery. *Medieval Arab Cookery: Essays and Translations.* Eds. Maxime Rodinson, A. J. Arberry, and Charles Perry. Blackawton, Totnes, Devon, U.K.: Prospect Books, 2006, 116-148.

Sherman, Sandra. *Invention of the Modern Cookbook.* Denver: Greenwood Press, 2010.

Spiller, Elizabeth. "Recipes for Knowledge: Maker's Knowledge and Traditions, Paraclesian Recipes, and the Invention of the Cookbook, 1600-1660." *Renaissance Food from Rabelais to Shakespeare: Culinary Readings and Culinary Histories.* Ed. Joan Fitzpatrick. Farnham: Ashgate, 2010, 55-72.

Thick, Malcolm. "Using Language to Investigate Ellen Chantrill's Recipe Book." *Food and Language: Proceedings of the Oxford Symposium on Food and Cookery 2009.* Ed. Richard Hosking. Blackawton, Totnes: Prospect Books, 2010, 350-359.

Van Winter, Johanna Maria. *Spices and Comfits: Collected Papers on Medieval Food.* Blackawton, Totnes, Devon, U.K.: Prospect Books, 2007.

Willan, Anne and Mark Cherniavsky. *The Cookbook Library: Four Centuries of the Cooks, Writers, and Recipes That Made the Modern Cookbook.* University of California Press, 2012.

Yoder, Don. "Historical Sources for American Traditional Cookery: Examples from the Pennsylvania German Culture." *Pennsylvania Folklife* 20 (3): 16-29, Spring 1971.

Wheaton, Barbara K. *Savoring the Past: The French Kitchen and Table from 1300 to 1789.* University of Pennsylvania Press, Philadelphia, 1983.

England, Culinary and General History:

Brears, Peter. *Cooking & Dining in Medieval England.* Blackawton, Totnes, Devon, U.K.: Prospect Books, 2008.

_____. *Cooking & Dining in Tudor & Early Stuart England.* Blackawton, Totnes, Devon, U.K.: Prospect Books, 2015.

Dawson, Mark. *Plenti and Grase: Food and Drink in a Sixteenth-Century Household.* Blackawton, Totnes, Devon, U.K.: Prospect Books, 2009.

Day, Ivan. "From Murrell to Jarrin: Illustrations in British Cookery Books, 1621–1820." Ed. Eileen White. *The English Cookery Book: Historical Essays.* Allaleigh House, Blackawthon, Totnes, Devon, U.K.: Prospect Books, 2004.

Eden, Trudy. *The Early American Table: Food and Society in the New World.* DeKalb: Northern Illinois University Press, 2008.

Elliott, John H. *Empires of the Atlantic World: Britain and Spain in America, 1942–1830.* New Haven: Yale University Press, 2007.

Hagen, Ann. *A Handbook of Anglo-Saxon Food: Processing and Consumption.* Pinner: Anglo-Saxon Books, 1992.

Hartley, Dorothy. *Food in England: A Complete Guide to the Food that Makes Us Who We Are*. London: Macdonald, 1954.

Mennell, Stephen. *All Manners of Food: Eating and Taste in England and France from the Middle Ages to the Present*. Oxford: Basil Blackwell, 1985.

Thirsk, Joan. *Food in Early Modern England: Phases, Fads, Fashions 1500–1760*. London: Hambledon Continuum, 2006.

Wall, Wendy. *Recipes for Thought: Knowledge and Taste in the Early Modern English Kitchen*. Philadelphia: University of Pennsylvania Press, 2016.

Wilson, C. Anne. *Food and Drink in Britain: From the Stone Age to the 19th Century*. Chicago: Academy Chicago Publishers, 1991.

Woolgar, C. M. *The Culture of Food in England, 1200–1500*. New Haven: Yale University Press, 2016.

Equipment and Material Culture of the Kitchen:

Braudel, Fernand. "*Histoire de la vie materielle*." Bulletin no. 2. *Alimentation et categories d'histoire. Annales: Economics, societs, civilizations* 16: 723-28, 1961.

Feild, Rachel. *Irons in the Fire: A History of Cooking Equipment*. Ramsbury: The Crowood Press, 1984.

Peachey, Stuart. *Cooking Techniques and Equipment, 1580–1660*. Volume 2. Bristol: Stuart Press, 1994.

Pennell, Sara. "Pots and Pans History": The Material Culture of the Kitchen in Early Modern England." *Journal of Design History* 11(3): 201-216, 1 January 1998.

Snodgrass, Mary Ellen. *Encyclopedia of Kitchen History*. Abingdon: Routledge, 2004.

Fire and Wood:

Adams, Margaret Byrd. *American Wood Heat Cookery*. 2nd edition. Seattle: Pacific Search Press, 1984.

Crump, Nancy Carter. *Hearthside Cooking: Early American Southern Cuisine Updated for Today's Hearth & Cookstove*. 2nd edition. Chapel Hill: University of North Carolina Press, 2008.

Goldenson, Suzanne and Doris Simpson. *The Open-Hearth Cookbook: Recapturing the Flavor of Early America*. Revised edition. Chambersburg, Pa: Alan C. Hood, 2006.

Harrison, Molly. *The Kitchen in History*. Reading: Osprey Publishing, 1972.

Hastie, Lennox. *Finding Fire: Cooking at its Most Elemental*. London: Hardie Grant Books, 2017.

Jaine, Tom. *Building a Wood-Fired Oven for Bread and Pizza*. Blackawton, Totnes, Devon, U.K.: Prospect Books, 1996.

Rubel, William. *The Magic of Fire: Hearth Cooking—One Hundred Recipes for the Fireplace or Campfire*. Berkeley: 10-Speed Press, 2002.

Wing, Daniel and Alan Scott. *The Bread Builders: Hearth Loaves and Masonry Ovens*. White River Junction, VT: Chelsea Green Publishing Company, 1999.

Wrangham, Richard W. *Catching Fire: How Cooking Made Us Human*. New York: Basic Books, 2009.

General History:

Adamson, Melitta Weiss. *Food in Medieval Times*. Westport, Conn.: Greenwood Press, 2004.

Appati, Alberto and Massimo Montinari. *Italian Cuisine: A Cultural History*. New York: Columbia University Press, 2003.

Flandrin, Jean-Louis and Massimo Montinari. *Food: A Culinary History*. New York: Columbia University Press, 1999.

Lambert, Carol. *Du Manuscrit à la Table (essais sur la cuisine au moyen age et repertoire des manuscrits medievaux contenant des recettes culunaires)*. Montreal: Les Presses de l'Université de Montréal, 1992.

Scully, D. Eleanor and Terence Scully. *Early French Cookery: Sources, History, Original Recipes and Modern Adaptations*. Ann Arbor: University of Michigan Press, 1996.

Scully, Terence. *The Art of Cookery in the Middle Ages*. Woodbridge: The Boydell Press, 1995.

Historiography and Historical Theory:

Authenticity in the Kitchen. Food and Communication: Proceedings from the 2005 Oxford Symposium on Food and Cookery. Ed. Richard Hosking. Blackawton, Totnes, Devon, U.K.: Prospect Books, 2006.

Claflin, Kyri W. and Peter Scholliers, eds. *Writing Food History: A Global Perspective*. Oxford: Berg Publishers, 2012.

Fischer, David Hackett. *Historians' Fallacies: Toward a Logic of Historical Thought*. York: HarperPerennial, 1970.

Harper, Laura Jane. "A Possible Framework for Studying Food in Culture." *The Virginia Culinary Thymes*. http://spec.lib.vt.edu/culinary/CulinaryThymes/2001 01/01Harper.html

Juarez Lopez, Jose Luis. *La lenta emergencia de la Comida Mexicana, ambiguedades criollas, 1750-1800*. Mexico: Miguel Angel Porrúa, 2005, 89.

Lévi-Strauss, Claude. *The Raw and the Cooked*. New York: Harper & Row, 1969.

Miller, Jeff and Jonathan Deutsch. *Food Studies: An Introduction to Research Methods*. Oxford: Berg, 2010.

Rippmann, Dorothee. " 'Take almaundes blaunched …' Cookbooks in the Middle Ages and Early Modern Times." Ed. Johannes Grabmeyer. *Culinary Art: History and Marketing.* CrossCulTour Summerschool, Friesach, Sept. 10 14, 2018.

http://crosscultour.uni-klu.ac.at/at/node/59

Schmidt, Stephen. "What Manuscript Cooks Can Tell Us that Printed Cookbooks Do Not." Manuscript Cookbooks Survey blog, May 2015.

http://www.manuscriptcookbookssurvey.org/essays/553/

_____. "When the West First Tasted the Cuisines of the East." Manuscript Cookbooks Survey blog, May 2018. http://www.manuscriptcookbookssurvey.org/when-the-west-first-tasted-the-cuisines-of-the-east/

Smith, Andrew F. "Culinary History: Toward a Conceptualization," *Culinary History.* Eds. A. Lynn Martin and Barbara Santich. Brompton, SA, Australia: East Street Publications, 2004, 1-13.

Spencer, Maryellen. "Food in Seventeenth-Century Tidewater Virginia: A Method for Studying Historical Cuisines." PhD dissertation. Virginia Polytechnic Institute and State University, 1982.

Wessell, Adele. "Cookbooks for Making History: As Sources for Historians and as Records of the Past." *M/C Journal* 16 (3), 2013.

http://journal.media-culture.org.au/index.php/mcjournal/article/view/717

Humoralism

Adamson, Melitta Weiss. *Medieval Dietetics: Food and Drink in "Regimen Sanitatis" Literature from 800 to 1400.* Frankfurt am Main: Peter Lang, 1995.

Albala, Ken. *Eating Right in the Renaissance.* Berkeley: University of California Press, 2002.

Earle, Rebecca. "Humoralism and the Colonial Body." *The Body of the Conquistador: Food, Race and the Colonial Experience in Spanish America, 1492–1700.* Cambridge University Press, Cambridge, 2012, 19-53.

Galen on Food and Diet. Ed. and Trans. Mark Grant. London: Routledge, 2000.

Scully, Terence. "The Theoretical Basis for Medieval Food and Cookery." *The Art of Cookery in the Middle Ages*. Woodbridge, Suffolk: The Boydell Press, 1995, 40-65.

Siraisi, Nancy G. *Medieval and Early Renaissance Medicine*. Chicago: University of Chicago Press, 1990.

Ingredients

Cowan, Brian. "New Worlds, New Taste: Food Fashion after the Renaissance." Ed. Paul Friedman. *The History of Taste*. Berkeley: University of California Press, 2007, 197-232.

Crosby, Alfred W. *The Columbian Exchange; Biological and Cultural Consequences of 1492*. Westport, Conn.: Greenwood Pub. Co., 1972.

Harvey, John H. "Vegetables in the Middle Ages." *Garden History* 12 (2): 89–99, 1984.

Kiple, Kenneth F, and Kriemhild C. Ornelas. *The Cambridge World History of Food*. Cambridge, UK: Cambridge University Press, 2000.

Schaefer, Hanno, et al. "Gourds Afloat: A Dated Phylogeny Reveals an Asian Origin of the Gourd Family (Cucurbitaceae) and Numerous Oversea Dispersal Events." *Proceedings: Biological Sciences* 276 (1658): 843–851, 2009.

Paleography, Plagiarism, Printing and Writing

Botein, Stephen. "The Anglo-American Book Trade before 1776: Personnel and Strategies." Eds. William L. Joyce et al. *Printing and Society in Early America*. Worcester: American Antiquarian Society, 1983.

Mennell, Stephen. "Plagiarism and Originality—Diffusionism in the Study of the History of Cooking." *Petits Propos Culinaires* 68: 29-38, 2001.

Notaker, Henry. "Comments on the Interpretation of Plagiarism." *Petits Propos Culinaires* 70: 58 – 66, 2002.

Santich, Barbara. "'Doing' Words: The Evolution of Culinary Vocabulary." *Food and Language: Proceedings from the 2009 Oxford Symposium on Food and Cookery*. Ed. Richard Hosking. Blackawton, Totnes, Devon, U.K.: Prospect Books, 2010, 301-310.

Stead, Jennifer. "Quizzing Glasse: Or Hannah Scrutinized, Part I." *Petits Propos Culinaires* 13: 9-24, 1983.

_____. "Quizzing Glasse: Or Hannah Scrutinized, Part II." *Petits Propos Culinaires* 14: 17-30, 1983.

Spain, Culinary and General History

Andrews, Coleman. *Catalan Cuisine: Europe's Last Great Culinary Secret.* Cambridge: Harvard Common Press, 1999.

Bertelsen, Cynthia D. "Sugar, Saffron, Spices: The Arab Influence on Spanish Cuisine, a Brief Meditation." *Gherkins & Tomatoes*, June 2, 2010.

https://gherkinstomatoes.com/2010/06/02/18078/

Campbell, Jodi. *At the First Table: Food and Social Identity in Early Modern Spain.* Lincoln: University of Nebraska Press, 2017.

Casas, Penelope. *The Foods & Wines of Spain.* New York: Knopf, 1983.

Chabran, Rafael. "Medieval Spain." *Regional Cuisines of Medieval Europe: A Book of Essays.* Ed. Melitta Weiss Adamson Routledge. New York. 2002, 125-152.

Dominguez, Fray Francisco Atanasio. *The Missions of New Mexico, 1776. A Description by Fray Francisco Atanasio Dominguez, with Other Contemporary Documents.* Eds. And Trans. Eleanor B. Adams and Fray Angelico Chavez. The University of New Mexico Press, Albuquerque, 1956, 311-312.

Earle, Rebecca. " 'If You Eat Their Food …': Diets and Bodies in Early Colonial Spanish America." *The American Historical Review* 115 (3): 688-713, 2010.

Elliott, John H. *Empires of the Atlantic World: Britain and Spain in America, 1942–1830.* New Haven: Yale University Press, 2007.

Fletcher, Richard. *Moorish Spain.* 2nd edition. Berkeley: University of California Press, 2006.

Freidenreich, David M. *Foreigners and their Food: Constructing Otherness in Jewish, Christian, and Islamic Law.* Berkeley: University of California Press, 2014.

Laudan, Rachel. "The Mexican Kitchen's Islamic Connections." *Saudi Aramco World,* 2004, 32-39.

Llopis, Manuel Martínez. *Historia de la gastronomia española.* Madrid: Editora Nacional, 1987.

Loreto López, Rosalva and Ana Benítez Muro. *Un Bocado para Los Ángeles: La Cocina Conventual Novohispana.* Mexico: Editorial Clío, 2000.

Luján, Nestor. *Historia de la gastronomia.* Barcelona: Folio, 1997.

Luján, Nestor y Juan Perucho. *El libro de la cocina Española: Gastronomia e historia.* Barcelona: Danae, 1970.

Selected Bibliographical Resources

Manjón, Maite. *The Gastronomy of Spain and Portugal*. New York: Prentice Hall, 1990.

Nadeau, Carolyn A. "The Author, the Reader, the Text: Literary Communication of a 1611 Spanish Cookbook." *Food and Communication: Proceedings from the 2009 Oxford Symposium on Food and Cookery*. Ed. Mark McWilliams. Blackawton, Totnes, Devon, U.K.: Prospect Books, 2016, 296-304.

_____. "Early Modern Spanish Cookbooks: The Curious Case of Diego Granado." *Food and Language: Proceedings from the 2015 Oxford Symposium on Food and Cookery*. Ed. Richard Hosking. Blackawton, Totnes, Devon, U.K.: Prospect Books, 2010, 237- 246.

_____. "Contributions of Medieval Food Manuals to Spain's Culinary Heritage." "Writing About Food: Culinary Literature in the Hispanic World." Ed. Maria Paz Moreno. Special issue. *Cincinnati Romance Review* 33: 59 – 67, 2012.

_____. *Food Matters: Alonso Quijano's Diet and the Discourse of Food in Early Modern Spain*. Toronto: University of Toronto Press, 2016.

Parry, J. H. *The Spanish Seaborne Empire*. Berkeley: University of California Press, 1990.

Peterson, Toby. "The Arab Influence on Western European Cooking." *Journal of Medieval* History 6: 317-341, 1980.

Reed, Maureen E. "Clinging to Tradition: Cleofas Jaramillo and the Transformed Home." *A Woman's Place: Women Writing New Mexico*. Ed. Maureen Reed. University of New Mexico Press, Albuquerque, N.M., 2005, 69-120.

_____ "Making Homes in a Changing Land: Fabiola Cabeza de Baca and the Double-Edged Present." *A Woman's Place: Women Writing New Mexico*. Ed. Maureen Reed. University of New Mexico Press, Albuquerque, N.M., 2005, 121-170.

Rios, Alicia and Lourdes Mardi. *The Heritage of Spanish Cooking*. New York: Random House, 1992.

Roden, Claudia. *A Book of Middle Eastern Food*. New York: Knopf, 1974.

_____. *The Food of Spain*. New York: Ecco, 2011.

Super, John, 1992. "Cookbooks and Culture in Early Latin America", paper presented at Simposio 1492: *El encuentro de dos comidas*, Puebla, Mexico. Printed as "Libras de Cocina y Cultura en la America Latina Temprana." Ed. Janet Long. *Conquista y Comida: Consequencias del encuentro de dos mundos*. Universidad Nacional Autonoma de Mexico, Mexico, 1996, 454.

Trigg, Heather B. "Food Choice and Social Identity in Early Colonial New Mexico." *Journal of the Southwest* 46 (2): 227, 2004.

_____. *From Household to Empire: Society and Economy in Early Colonial Mexico*. Tucson: University of Arizona Press, 2005.

Wilson, C. Anne. "The Saracen Connection: Arab Cuisine and the Mediaeval West." *Petits Propos Culinaires* 7: 13-22 and 8: 19-27, 1981.

Zaouali, Lilia. *Medieval Cuisine of the Islamic World.* Berkeley: University of California Press, 2009.

Writing Fiction, and Culinary History

Bertelsen, Cynthia D. "Avoid Cringeworthy Culinary Anachronisms in Your Historical Fiction." Writers Alliance of Gainesville, January 17, 2018.

https://writersalliance.org/avoid-cringeworthy-culinary-anachronisms/

Brayfield, Celiua and Duncan Sprott. Writing Historical Fiction: A Writer's and Artist's Companion. London: Bloomsbury, 2014.

Foreng, Jeffrey L. *Daily Life in Elizabethan England.* Santa Barbara, Calif.: Greenwood Press, 2018.

Gies, Joseph and Frances Gies. *Life in a Medieval City.* New York: Harper Perennial, 1969.

Goodman, Ruth. *How to be a Tudor.* New York: Liveright Publishing Corp., 2015.

Illustrations

With the exception of copyright-free book covers and examples of their text, all illustrations are the copyrighted work of Courtney Nzeribe.

Index

Page numbers in italics refer to illustrations.

A

The Accomplisht Cook (May), 34, 50, 150–155
Achatz, Grant, 15
action words, in cookbook analysis, 71, *74*
aesch (ash), 68
Age of Exploration, 57, 73. *See also* Columbian Exchange
aides-mémoires, cookbooks as, 42–43, 46, 73, 97
Allen, Darina, 82
Allen, Gary, 15
Altamiras, Juan, 57, 122–128
American Cookery (Simmons), 52
Andrews, Coleman, 82
Annals of the Caliphs' Kitchens (Nasrallah), 82
Anonymous Andalusian (*Kitâb al-Tabîkh fi'l-Maghrib wa'l Andalus fi'asr al-Muwahhidin),* 20, 53
Arab influence on cookbooks, 20, 43, 47–48, 53–57
archaeological resources, online, 61-62, 72, 169
Arte cisoria: arte de trinchar o cortar con cuchillo carnes y demás viandas (Villena), 56
Arte de cocina, pasteleria, vizcocheria, y conservia (Art of Cooking, Pastry, Savory Pastry and Preserves) (Martínez Montiño), 56, 57, 115-121
Arte de reposteria (Mata), 57
Art of Cookery: A Spanish Friar's Kitchen Notebook (Hayward), 127. *See also* Altamiras, Juan

The Art of Cookery, Made Plain and Easy (Glasse), 26, 51, 156–160
The Art of Cookery (Maestro Martino), 112
art resources, online, 169
ashes, importance for cooking fires, 87
authenticity, definition of culinary, 67
Avicenna, 38
Avoirdupois weights (modern American), 81

B

Barros, Cristina, 180n36
Beeton, Isabella, 44
Berejenas ala Morisca (Eggplants Aubergines Moorish Style), 103–107
bibliographies, reasons for, 165-168
bile, 38. *See also* humoral theory
Bilyk, Marcia Krause, 15
blood, 38. *See also* humoral theory
A Booke of Cookrye (A. W.), 50
Book of Household Management (Beeton), 44
A Book of Middle Eastern Food (Roden), 82
The Book of Sent Soví, 69, 94-99
Bradley, Martha, 44, 51, 70–71
Branciaroli, Cathy, 15
Briggs, Richard, 52
The British Housewife (Bradley), 44, 51, 70–71
The British Housewife (Lehmann), 146

C

calendars, online resources, 174
capirotada, 116–121
    modern version *versus* Francisco
    Martínez Montiño's, 75
Casas, Penelope, 82, 97, 120
Catalan Cuisine (Andrews), 82
Catalonia, 54–55. *See also* Nola,
    Ruperto de; *Sent Sovi*
*Catching Fire: How Cooking Made Us
    Human* (Wrangham), 85
Catholic Monarchs, 46, 179–180n25
chinois, definition of, 180n37
"closet," definition of, 51
*The Closet Of Sir Kenelm Digby
    Knight, Opened* (Digby), 50, 51
collective nouns, definition of, 11
color, importance in cooking, 39-40,
    81, 146
The Columbian Exchange, 44, 46.
    See also Age of Exploration; Spain
Columbus, Christopher, 46
The Compleat Housewife (Smith), 26
complexion, 39, 41. *See also* humoral
    theory
Com usar de beure e menjar (Francesc
    Eiximenis), 54
confits verus comfits, 146
conversos, 55
cookbooks
    as *aides-mémoires,* 42–43, 46, 73,97
    authors of, male *versus* female,
        42–44, 46, 51
    for basics, online resources, 170
    definitions of, 29–30
    digitized online resources, 170
    literacy and, 37, 44
    medicine and, 37–41, 43. *see also*
        humoral theory
    modern, as resources in recipe
        reconstruction, 82
    plagiarism and, 30, 51, 75
    role in historical research, 31–32,
        62–63
    step-by-step analysis, 67–75
    types of, 42, 46
cookstoves, 181n39
Crump, Nancy Carter, 89
culinary authenticity, definition of, 67
culinary history, methodology,
    61–63, 65–66, 172
Cusack, Igor, 180n36

D

Dawson, Thomas, 44
definitions
    of authenticity, 67
    of bibliographies, 167–168
    of chinois, 180n37
    of "closet," 51
    of coffin, 134
    of collective nouns, 11
    of confits and comfits, 146
    of cookbooks, 29–30
    of cooking, 178n9
    of culinary authenticity, 67
    of "cury," 48
    of A Hastiness of Cooks, 11
    of messes, 134
    of sotelties, 48, 134
De Honesta voluptate (Platina), 32
De Humani Corporis Fabrica
    (Vesalius), 39
*The Delights of the Table (Fudalat
    al-Khiwan),* 20
De Pollos Rellenos (Stuffed
    Chickens), 110–113
dictionaries, online resources,
    170–171
doctrine of signatures, 39, 41. *See
    also* humoral theory
doctrine of similarities, 39. *See also*
    humoral theory

document and title page analysis, online resources, 171

Douce MS 257, 134

To Dress a Loin of Pork with Onions, 158–160

Dutch ovens, 89

E

The Elements of Cooking: Translating the Chef's Craft for Every Kitchen (Ruhlman), 82

empires, 20–21. *See also* England; Spain

England, historic cookbooks in, 47–52. *See also* specific authors and cookbook titles

The English Art of Cookery (Briggs), 52

English Food (Grigson), 73, 82

The English Hus-wife (Markham), 26, 50, 142–149

Enumerative Bibliography, 168

equipment, for recipe reconstruction, 71–72, 78–79, 88–89

online resources, 171

Evard, Mary, 181n39

The Experienced English Housekeeper (Raffald), 51

F

fasting days, 31, 38, 42, 55

fats, role of, 81

Fettiplace, Elinor, 50

final dishes, appearance and serving details, 74–75

fire, in recreating historic recipes, 85–89

basic composition of, 88

best type of wood for, *86*, 86–87

"heat feel," 87–88, *88*

Fish *sikbāj*, 97

flavors, in Western Europe cuisine,

20, 39, 41, 48, 74, 81, 184, 185

flesh days, 42

Food (Hume), 62

Food in England (Hartley), 82

The Food of Spain (Roden), 73, 82

food preparation, basic steps for, 73–74

The Foods & Wines of Spain (Casas), 82, 120

Forgotten Skills of Cooking: the Time Honored Ways are the Best – Over 700 Recipes Show You the Way (Allen), 82

form, for recipe reconstruction, 78, 188–189

The Forme of Cury, 20, 47–48, 68, 130–135

four humors, 38–39. *See also* humoral theory

France, 47, 50, 177n3. *See also* specific authors and cookbook titles

Francesc Eiximenis, 54

Fritters of Spinage, 153–155

frontispieces, analysis of, 69–70

The Frugal Housewife, or, Complete Woman Cook (Carter), 52

Fudalat al-Khiwan (The Delights of the Table), 20

G

Galen, 38, 179n19

The Gastronomy of Spain and Portugal (Manjón), 82

Glasse, Hannah, 26, 51, 156–160

glossaries, online resources, 172

The good Huswifes Handmaide for the Kitchin, 139

Google, 105, 165

Granado, Diego de, 57

Grigson, Jane, 73, 82

guilds, 31, 178n11, 181n47

Index

H

haravillo, 104, 105
Hartley, Dorothy, 82
Harvey, William, 39
Hayward, Vicky, 127, 180n36
hearth cooking, 85–86. *See also* fire, in recreating historic recipes
"heat feel," 87–88, *88*
Henry IV of England, 48
Hernández de Maceras, Domingo, 56, 108–113
Hess, Karen, 41, 52, 120
Hippocrates, 38, 179n19
Hollinsworth, Arthur, 50, 151
Hume, Audrey Noel, 62
Hume, Ivor, 62
humoral theory, 38–41, *40*, 43, 46

I

Ibn Sayyer al-Warraq, 55
indexing, importance in databases,. 166
ingredients. *See also* flavors, in Western Europe cuisine
flavors and, 72–73
online resources, 172
Italy, 53, 177n3. *See also* specific authors and cookbook titles

J

Jaine, Tom, 33
Johnson, Samuel, 42, 179n23
Joy of Cooking (Rombauer), 73, 82, 140

K

Kernan, Sarah Peters, 42, 47
King Henry of Portugal, 46
Kirkpatrick, David, 15
Kirkpatrick, Meli Duran, 15
Kitâb al-Tabîkh fi'l-Maghrib wa'l Andalus fi'asr al-Muwahhidin (Anonymous Andalusian), 20, 53
Kitab al-Tabîkh (The Book of Dishes) (Ibn Sayyer al-Warraq), 55
kitchens, organization of, 41–42, 48, 65, 69, 72
Kowalchuk, Kristine, 19
Kranmer, Keith, 41

L

La Cocinera Poblana, 57
La cuisiniere bourgeoise (Menon), 44
Laudan, Rachel, 15
Lehmann, Gilly, 146
Le livre du cuisinier de l'eveche de Tarragone, 54
Le Ménagier de Paris, 44
Leonard, Ria, 15
Lévi-Strauss, Claude, 73
Liber cure cocorum, 134
Libra del arte de cocina (Granado), 57
libraries, containing culinary history collections, 172–173
Libre de Sent Soví, 54
Libre de totes maneres de confits, 55, 56
Libro del Arte de Cozina (Hernández de Maceras), 56, 108-113
literacy, 178n16
cookbooks and, 37, 71
European history, online resources, 173
female, 44, 49
Llibre del coch (Book of the Cook) (Nola), 55
Llibre de Sent Soví., 20
The London Art of Cookery (Farley), 52
long "s," 68

M

macrons, 68
Maestro Martino, 112
The Magic of Fire (Rubel), 88
To Make Pyes of Grene Apples, 138–141

Manjón, Maite, 82
Manual de mugeres en el cual se contienen muchas y diversas recetas muy buenas, 55
Markham, Gervase, 26, 50, 73, 142–149, 159, 177n6
Martínez Montiño, Francisco, 56, 57, 75, 114–121, 177n4
Mata, Juan de la, 57
May, Robert, 50, 51, 150–155, 159
measurements, 81, 173
medicine. *See also* humoral theory
  cookbooks and, 37–41, 43
  online resources, 174
Medieval Cuisine of the Islamic World (Zaouali), 97
Mediterranean Vegetables (Wright), 105
Mennell, Stephen, 42, 179n24
Menon, 44
menu collections, online resources, 174
Merriam-Webster's Collegiate Dictionary, 29
Mestre Robert, 55–56, 100–107, 180n34
money units, online resources, 173

N

Nadeau, Carolyn A., 120, 177n4
National Trust cookbooks, 82
The Neapolitan Recipe Collection (Cuoco Napoletano), 43
Neville, George, 48
Newton, Isaac, 180n28
A Noble Boke Off Cookry, 48, 134
Nola, Ruperto de, 55–56, 100–107, 180n34
Notaker, Henry, 29, 30
Nuevo arte de cocina, 57, 122-128
Nzeribe, Courtney, 15

O

Old English writing, 68. *See also* paleography
"Old Woman Frying Eggs," 127
Olla Podrida, 75, 118, 120
Online Tools, 169–174
Opera (Scappi), 44
Ortiz-Díaz, Lourdes, 180n36
Oxford English Dictionary, 29

P

paleography, 68, 174
pantry, for recipe reconstruction, 78–81
Parks, William, 26
Pegge, Samuel, 68
Peposo, 126
Pérez Dávila, 101
Perlman, Janet, 15
phlegm, 38. *See also* humoral theory
pierna, discussion of, 112
pipkins, 181n45
pippins, 140
plagiarism, cookbooks and, 30, 38, 51, 52, 55, 75
Platina (Bartolomeo Sacchi di Piadena), 32, 39
Pollack, Liz, 15
Pollos de Carretero, con Salsa de Pobres (Chicken in the Style of Carreteros, with Peppery "Poor Man's" Sauce), 125–128
Poudre Blanche, 80
Poudre Doux/Poudre Fine, 79, 81
Poudre Forte, 79, 134
printing press, importance of invention of, 37–38, 47
A Proper Newe Booke of Cokerye, 49, 123-128, 136–141
protein sources in Western Europe, 187
Puddings of the Hogges Liuer, 50

Q

The Queen-Like Closet (Woolley), 42

R

Raffald, Elizabeth, 51
Ratio: The Simple Codes Behind the Craft of Everyday Cooking (Ruhlman), 82
The Raw and the Cooked (Strauss), 73
recipe reconstruction. *See also* flavors, in Western Europe cuisine
   basics of, 77–82
   common techniques in, 81
   equipment for, 78–79, 88–89
   fire in, 85–89
   form for, 78, 188–189
   modern cookbooks as resources for, 82
   spices used in, 79–80
recipes
   Berejenas ala Morisca (Eggplants Aubergines Moorish Style), 103–107
   Capirotada, 116–121
   Capitol CLI. Qui parla con se deuen coura albergines en casola, 105
   Capouns In Councys, 132–135
   De Pollos Rellenos (Stuffed Chickens), 110–113
   To Dress a Loin of Pork with Onions, 158–160
   Fritters of Spinage, 153–155
   To Make Pyes of Grene Apples, 138–141
   Pollos de Carretero, con Salsa de Pobres (Chicken in the Style of Carreteros, with Peppery "Poor Man's" Sauce), 125–128
   Poudre Blanche, 80
   Poudre Doux/Poudre Fine, 79, 81
   Poudre Forte, 79, 134
   A Prune Tart, 144–149
   Si Vols Fer Escabetx (If You Wish to Make Escabeche), 95–99
Reedy, Cathy Gibbons, 15
Reliance Cook Stove, 181n39
Robertson, Laurel, 15
Roden, Claudia, 73, 82
Roman Catholic Church, 55. *See also* fasting days
Roman cuisine, 53
Rombauer, Irma, 73, 82
rounded r, 68
Rubel, William, 88
Ruhlman, Michael, 82
Rylands manuscript, 134

S

Sacchi di Piadena, Bartolomeo, 32, 39
safety issues, in cooking with fire, 89
sauces, 81, 180–181n38
Savoring the Past: The French Kitchen and Table from 1300 to 1789 (Wheaton), 33
Sawse Blaunche, 68
Scandinavia, 47
Scappi, Bartolomeo, 44
Scopus (Elsevier), 166
Scott, Elizabeth M., 33
Scully, Terence, 37, 42
Sent Soví, 20, 54, 55, 56, 69, 94–99, 105
Shakespeare, William, 144
Siglo de Oro, 57
Simmons, Amelia, 52
Si Vols Fer Escabetx (If You Wish to Make Escabeche), 95–99
Sloane manuscript, 48, 134
Smith, E., 26, 178n7
sotelties, definition of, 48, 134
Spain. *See also* specific authors and cookbook titles
   Arab influence on cuisine of, 20,

47-48, 55
historic cookbooks in, 53–57
Spencer, Maryellen, 61–62
spices, Venice and, 41. *See also*
    flavors, in Western Europe
    cuisine
Spurling, Hilary, 50
step-by-step analysis, of cookbooks,
    67–75
Stuffed Chickens *(De Pollos
    Rellenos),* 110–113
Subject Bibliography, 168
sweetening, in cooking, 81

T

Tacuinum Sanitatis (Ibn Butlan of
    Baghdad), 43
Taillevent (Guillaume Tirel), 42
tart flavors, in cooking, 81
texture, in cooking, 7
thorn, Old English letter, 68, 133
The Three Ts, 67–69
tildes, 68, 112
timelines
    English cooking, *49*
    online resources, 174
    Spanish cooking, *54*
Tirel, Guillaume (Taillevent), 42
title pages, analysis of, 69–70
*Traite historique et pratique de la
    cuisine. Ou le cuisinier instruit*
    (Menon), 44
transcription, 69
translation, 69
transliteration, 68
Troy/apothecary weights
    (medieval), 81
Tyler, R., 29

U

Utilis Coquinario, 48

V

Vargas, Diego de, 25, *27,* 57
vegetables, in Western Europe, 186
Venice, 41
verjuice (verjus), 68, 80, 81, 105, 126,
    181n43
Vesalius, Andreas, 39
Villena, Enrique de, 56

W

weights, online resources, 173
Wheaton, Barbara Ketchum, 15,
    32–33
Willan, Anne, 41
wood, best types for cooking with
    fire, *86,* 86–87
Woolgar, C. M., 11
Woolley, Hannah, 42
Worshipful Company of Cooks,
    181n47
Wrangham, Richard, 85
Wright, Clifford, 105
writing styles, online resources, 174

Y

yogh, Old English letter, 68

Z

Zaouali, Lilia, 97

About The Author

An avid cook and cookbook collector, Cynthia D. Bertelsen is a food historian, photographer, and compulsive writer now settled in Gainesville, Florida. She lived and worked long-term in Mexico, Paraguay, Honduras, Haiti, Morocco and Burkina Faso. Her book, *Mushroom: A Global History*, appeared in 2013, published by Reaktion Books UK. Cynthia's articles and book reviews have appeared in several well-known food-studies encyclopedias, journals, and newspapers, including *Gastronomica* and *The Oxford Encyclopedia of American Food and Drink* (2nd edition). In 2011, she won a Julia Child Independent Scholar grant from the International Association of Culinary Professionals to study the impact of France's colonial heritage on the future of French cuisine. For more of Cynthia's writing, read her blog "Gherkins and Tomatoes," brimming with in-depth analyses of cooking, cookbooks, and food history.

About The Illustrator

The books that fascinated Courtney Nzeribe the most as a child were those with rich illustrations of some culinary concoction or pastry. Courtney studied Fashion Design at Parsons School of Design Paris, France. Ultimately, she ended up in the cosmetic retail profession as an Account Executive, painting faces and managing territories throughout the Midwest, Canada, and the Caribbean. Never abandoning her dual culinary aspirations, she worked as a self-taught personal chef for local clientele and Chicago's diplomatic Consular community. Art and all things culinary are mediums Courtney intertwines via illustrations and paintings. She has written for publications such as *Ebony, EbonyJet.com*, and her food blog: "Coco Cooks," gaining inspiration from her extensive travels and culinary adventures. *A Hastiness of Cooks* is her first role as illustrator for a book, combining her myriad interests. Courtney currently resides in Chicago with her long-term partner Marc.